The EU Pregnancy Directive

To Tim

The EU Pregnancy Directive

A Guide for Human Resource Managers

HELEN COLLINS

BLACKWELL
Business

First published 1994

Blackwell Publishers
108 Cowley Road
Oxford OX4 1JF
UK

238 Main Street,
Cambridge, Massachusetts 02142
USA

British Library Cataloguing in Publication Data

A CIP catalogue record for this book is available from the British Library.

Library of Congress Cataloging-in-Publication Data

Collins, Helen.
The EU pregnancy directive: a guide for human resource managers / Helen Collins.
p. cm.
Includes index.
ISBN 0-631-19371-5
1. Maternity leave—Government policy—European Union countries. 2. Parental leave—Government policy—European Union countries. 3. Work and family—Government policy—European Union countries. 4. Pregnant women—Employment—Law and legislation—European Union countries. 5. Maternity leave—Government policy—Great Britain. 6. Parental leave—Government policy—Great Britain. 7. Work and family—Government policy—Great Britain. 8. Pregnant women—Employment—Law and legislation—Great Britain. I. Title.
HD6065.5.E86C65 1994
331.4'4—dc20 93-48398
CIP

Typeset in 11 on 13 pt Plantin by Best-set Typesetter Ltd., Hong Kong

Printed and Bound in Great Britain by Hartnolls Limited, Bodmin, Cornwall.

This book is printed on acid-free paper

Contents

Preface

The purpose of this book

There is now an extensive range of literature available covering most areas in the field of women's employment issues. However, there has not yet been any detailed and comprehensive study of the different initiatives on pregnancy and employers' responsibilities to their employees in respect of maternity, paternity and parental rights. This guide fills that gap. Information concerning parental rights as well as childcare provision and family benefits in member states has been presented as objectively as possible within national contexts; in view of the wide range of employment, social and welfare structures, any attempts at comparison would have forced a subjective bias, which would be counter to the book's aim to provide the facts and not assumptions about each country.

Who is it for?

The guide is intended to serve human resource managers, advisers and consultants, trainers and employers as well as employees and students.

How to use the book

Part I provides information about the EU pregnancy directive and what it means for employers and employees; advice on European funding and childcare, and information and guidance on the development of organizational policies in the fields of parental responsibilities and childcare. A final chapter in this section considers the advantages to employers of flexible working patterns.

In Part II all the country chapters follow the same model and are organized into nine subsections:

- Statutory maternity provision
- Statutory paternity provision
- Statutory parental provision
- Leave for family reasons
- Childbirth grants or maternity allowances
- Family benefits
- Publicly funded childcare provision
- Health matters
- Information points

Given the constant changes and developments in employment in the European Union, no guide of this nature can ever be absolutely complete; the final section, 'Information Points', therefore gives readers the opportunity to find out more about any particular aspect. A glossary of terms, summary of EU legal measures, EU information points and a pregnancy checklist for employers and employees are provided in appendices at the back of the book.

Helen Collins

List of Abbreviations

ACAS	Advisory, Conciliation and Arbitration Service
BAECE	British Association for Early Childhood Education
CBI	Confederation of British Industry
COFACE	Confederation of Family Organizations in the EU
COREPER	Committee of Permanent Representatives
CREW	Centre for Research into European Women
DSS	Department of Social Security
EAGGF	European Agricultural Guidance and Guarantee Fund
ECJ	European Court of Justice
EIC	European Information Centre
EOC	Equal Opportunities Commission
EPA	Equal Pay Act
EP(C)A	Employment Protection (Consolidation) Act
ERDF	European Regional Development Fund
ESF	European Social Fund
EU	European Union
EURO COOP	European Confederation of Consumer Co-operatives
EUROFEDOP	European Federation of Employers in Public Services
FAS	The Employment and Training Authority (Ireland)
INPS	National Institute for Social Security (Italy)
IPM	Institute of Personnel Management
NCC	National Consumer Council
NHS	National Health Service
NOW	New Opportunities for Women
OAED	Greek Manpower Employment Organization
PSRI	Pay-related Social Insurance (Ireland)

SCAFA	Scottish Child and Family Alliance
SDA	Sex Discrimination Act
SMP	Statutory Maternity Pay
SSP	Statutory Sick Pay
TEC	Training and Enterprise Council
TEED	Training, Enterprise and Education Directorate
TUC	Trades Union Congress
UNICE	Union of Industrial and Employers Confederation of Europe
VDU	Visual Display Unit
VOLCUF	Voluntary Organizations Liaison Council for Under Fives

PART I

Pregnancy, Parental Rights and Responsibilities, Childcare: the Issues for Employers

1

Background: The 'Common Position' of the EU Pregnancy Directive

The economic prosperity and social welfare of a region, in this case the European Union, largely depend on the level of training of its citizens, their social as much as their vocational competence, and above all on their ability and willingness to learn and adapt to new situations. The growing Europeanization of markets, firms, vocational qualifications, products and services indicates that the development of a Union component for industry-led, family-friendly policies is likely to be highly beneficial.

Above all, however, it is the firms themselves, as the core institutions of economic activity, and as competitors in a free-market system, that lay the foundations for their competitiveness and innovativeness and for their ability to cooperate beyond national frontiers by training their personnel. The special interest that practitioners, academics and politicians have been taking in the implementation of parental employment policies has been primarily due to a number of factors. These factors include demographic changes, women's increasing contribution to the paid labour market, the changing face of industry, not to mention the growing leverage and acceptance of feminist ideology which underpins all progress in the field of equality.

In general, the emphasis is tending to shift, to a greater or lesser degree, from physical to human capital, depending on the firm and specific national culture. In post-industrial society, the firm is increasingly becoming more than just a technical, economic and organizational unit for the provision of economic services which, though shaped by human beings, has to be served by most of them in accordance with prescribed performance requirements and expectations. We know today, however, that the success of a firm depends above all on people, and not primarily on their functionality and their 'functioning', but on their goals and expectations, on enabling and encouraging them to experience work as a worthwhile activity, on their satisfaction and on the development of their strengths. Viewed from this angle, organizational development and personnel development are integrative elements of an interdependent process which obeys a basic principle pervading all a firm's departments: the firm as a learning environment. This is a vision and increasingly a fact. With the emergence of new corporate identities that hinge on participation and on co- and self-responsibility, learning in the firms is also changing to some extent, becoming a process that initially develops more or less spontaneously, but also needs to be consciously and deliberately promoted. At the same time, these changes of climate in the firms and the world of work are accompanied by specific changes:

- in the requirements and organization of work (reduction of the division of labour and combination of individual activities, formation of semi-autonomous or autonomous working groups to replace individual workplaces, enlargement and differentiation of areas of responsibility, reduction in the number of hierarchical levels in the structure of tasks and the work-force, etc.);
- in skill requirements (object-orientated skills are increasingly giving way to process-orientated skills. Functional directing skills are replacing specifically operative skills. Traditional social virtues are not being displaced, but complemented to a very large degree by social competence. The isolated performance of functions is giving way to co-operative and self-determined work. The continuous performance of accurately defined tasks is increasingly being replaced by variable structuring of work and performance of tasks).

The question is whether these and other changes should continue to take place at national level and at the level of individual firms, or whether there should be a more purposeful and wider-scale effort, using supranational family and workplace training, to make workplace practices better reflect family concerns and to encourage more organizations to address this problem. It must also be recalled in this context that employees who are also parents form a very large group of people with a varied multiplier effect, whether they are heads of in-company or out-of-company training centres, whether they are full time or part time, etc. In the end there is something to be said for the assumption that the growing Europeanization of the economies of the European Union is bound to have implications for the career profiles of this group of people. In other words it should be considered whether the qualification requirements to be satisfied by future workers should not be enriched by European components through a form of continuing training towards totally integrated workplace family policies which, on the one hand, takes account of new conditions and requirements and, on the other hand, is likely to promote the 'Europeanization' of parent-friendly workplace practices, and thus of the economy.

The EU Directive

In October 1992 the Council of Ministers adopted a directive on the introduction of measures to encourage improvements in the safety and health at work of pregnant workers and workers who have recently given birth or are breastfeeding. The directive was proposed in the Commission's Action Programme implementing the EU Charter of basic social rights for workers and originally put forward on 12 September 1990. It is the tenth individual directive within the meaning of Article 16 (1) of the Framework Directive 89/391/EEC and its provisions will thus apply not only to employees, but also to trainees and apprentices. There are currently 52 million women workers in the European Union. The directive followed concerns over the falling European population and shortages of skilled workers. The Commission felt that it had proposed the minimum requirements that were necessary to protect the health of pregnant women and their foetuses, without reducing women's employment opportunities.

The Commission believed that there were discrepancies between member states' provisions for pregnant workers; for example, maternity leave ranged from 12 weeks in the Netherlands to 40 in the UK (although pay is not always included for the full period). Further, some member states prohibited night work whilst others allowed it in certain occupations.

The progress of the directive had always been controversial, and when the European Commission unexpectedly accepted 11 of the 17 amendments (more than had been anticipated) from the European Parliament's May 1992 second reading, it appeared as if the directive would never be adopted. The amendments entailed many changes in practice; they included improved protection on night work and a restoration of the link between maternity pay and normal, rather than sick pay.

The problems arose because the return to the December 1991 'common position' would have required a unanimous vote but Italy was in disagreement. Final agreement was reached after an informal Social Affairs Council meeting; further work by the Committee of Permanent Representatives (COREPER) resulted in a return to the common position form with three amendments:

- the addition of a final recital, stating that although the 'adequate allowance' for maternity leave was based on sick pay, under no circumstances was there an analogy between pregnancy and sickness;
- member states to report on the practical implementation four years after adoption;
- the Council of Ministers to assess the reports of member states and, if necessary, to draw up a further proposal five years after adoption, at the latest.

The common position version of the pregnancy directive was adopted on the 19 October 1992, after two extensions of the deadline. The final irony was that the UK, which had initiated the amendments to break the deadlock, abstained at the final vote as it disputed the legal basis of the directive. Italy also abstained, in protest at what it considered an insufficient maternity allowance. A declaration was included that the link with sick pay was a 'technical' point, and was not meant to imply that pregnancy was an illness.

It is expected that member states will provide a report on progress four years after adoption and that in the fifth year a review will take place and the European Commission may then consider what other measures (if any) are required. Member states are obliged to implement the directive by October 1994. Each country's government has to introduce new legislation or adapt existing laws to take into account the main points of the directive. In the UK the vehicle for implementation of the directive is the Employment Bill, which received its second reading in the House of Commons on 17 November 1992.

The main points of the directive can be summarized as follows:

Maternity leave All pregnant women are to be given a period of at least 14 weeks' maternity leave irrespective of length of service and hours of work, allocated before or after confinement; this must include compulsory leave of at least two weeks allocated before or after confinement. It is questionable whether many women will be able to exercise a right to return after only 14 weeks because much, if not all their leave entitlement could have to be taken before childbirth, or may be needed to accommodate cases of multiple or premature births or births where there have been medical complications.

Assessment Employers must assess the nature, degree and duration of exposure for all activities which are likely to involve a specific risk of exposure to agents, processes or working conditions including:

- *Physical agents*: those regarded as causing foetal lesions or likely to disrupt placental attachment, particularly: shocks, vibration or movement; handling of loads entailing risks; noise; ionizing radiation; non-ionising radiation; extremes of cold or heat; movements or postures; travelling; and mental and physical fatigue;
- *Certain biological agents*: risk groups 2, 3 and 4 within the meaning of Directive 90/679/EEC, insofar as it is known that they endanger the health of the woman or foetus;
- *Certain chemical agents*: substances labelled R40, R45 and R47; chemical agents in annex 1 to Directive 90/394/EEC; mercury and mercury derivatives.

Protection against dismissal There will be a prohibition against dismissal for a period from the beginning of pregnancy to the end of maternity leave, save in exceptional cases not connected with pregnancy or maternity. Employers have to provide written reasons for the dismissal of an employee if it takes place during pregnancy or maternity leave, and member states must take measures necessary to provide protection from unlawful dismissal.

Contractual rights During maternity leave all contractual rights are to be maintained.

Health and safety and EU guidelines The European Commission, following consultation, will draw up guidelines on the assessment of chemical, physical and biological agents, and industrial processes considered hazardous for the safety or health of pregnant workers. The guidelines should cover a whole range of potential problems that might affect these women including:

- movements and postures;
- mental and physical fatigue;
- physical stress;
- chemical, physical and biological agents and industrial processes.

Member states are to bring these guidelines to the attention of employers and all female workers.

The directive contains a list of agents, processes and working conditions which involve risks to the health and safety of pregnant and breastfeeding women. Employers will be obliged to assess the nature, degree and duration of exposure to these risks in their workplaces and decide what measures should be taken. Employees are to be informed of the risk assessment activities as well as the conclusions that are drawn from them.

If the results of a risk assessment exercise reveal a risk, employers must take the following steps to minimize risk and avoid further exposure to the danger, hazard or risk.

- The employer should temporarily adjust the working conditions or working hours of the employee.
- If this is not feasible, the employee should be moved to another job.
- If this is not possible, the employee should be granted leave for the whole of the period necessary for her protection. All contractual employment rights, including those relating to pay and entitlement to an adequate allowance, are to be maintained during the period of leave.

The directive contains a list of agents and working conditions to which pregnant or breastfeeding women must not be exposed in any circumstances, for example, underground mining work, underwater diving, exposure to rubella, toxoplasma, salmonellosis, lead. Full contractual rights, including those relating to pay and adequate allowance are to be maintained during periods of leave taken to avoid exposure to these risks.

Night work Women who are pregnant or breastfeeding or have recently given birth are not to perform night work if they provide a medical certificate stating that this is necessary for their health and safety. These workers are to be transferred to daytime work or, if this is not feasible, to be granted leave from work or extension of maternity leave with no loss of employment rights.

Eligibility of maternity pay

- Maintenance of a payment or entitlement to an adequate allowance, or both, are to be guaranteed during maternity leave. This payment or allowance is to be at least equivalent to that which the employee would receive in the event of absence from work for health reasons.

- Member states may introduce eligibility criteria for the above; these should not include a requirement for periods of previous employment in excess of 12 months immediately prior to the presumed date of confinement.
- All pregnant women are to be entitled to paid time off work for antenatal examinations, if such examinations have to take place during working hours.

2

The Pregnancy Directive: Potential Impact in Britain

An estimated 380,000 British women a year are in paid employment while pregnant. The proposal to entitle all women, irrespective of hours they work or length of service, to 14 weeks' maternity leave will benefit approximately 150,000 women a year in Great Britain (that is, the 40 per cent of employed pregnant women who do not qualify under the existing arrangements). The biggest gainers will be:

- women who work part time: almost 90 per cent of pregnant women working between 8 and 16 hours per week, approximately 30,000, are excluded each year by the current arrangements. Also excluded are all pregnant women working fewer than 8 hours per week; that number is approximately 10,000 women;
- women working in unskilled and semi-skilled jobs.

British women stop working on average 11 weeks before the birth and return to work on average 20 weeks after the birth. While this pattern is influenced to an extent by statutory entitlement, other factors, such as the absence in the UK of parental and paternity leave (the UK and Ireland are the only two member states not to have some form of statutory parental leave) and a low level of publicly funded childcare provision, also play a major role. It is therefore doubtful that, without substantial changes also occurring in the provision of childcare and paternity or parental leave, many women will be able to exercise a right to return to work after only 14 weeks' leave.

Protection against dismissal

The largest benefactors from the proposal to prohibit dismissal on the grounds of pregnancy will be women working in unskilled and semi-skilled jobs, who are twice as likely as managerial and professional women to experience dismissal. An estimated 4,000 women are dismissed or forced to resign each year on the grounds of pregnancy. Reasons vary: some are simply dismissed without any justifiable explanation, others are forced to resign through their employer's reluctance to allow them time off to attend antenatal appointments, while others are engaged in unsuitable jobs which carry a high health risk to a pregnant woman and her employer is unable or unwilling to transfer her to more suitable employment for the duration of pregnancy.

In future employers will be required to give written reasons for any dismissal during pregnancy and maternity. However, employers rarely admit that pregnancy is the reason for dismissal. In order to overcome this difficulty, the Equal Opportunities Commission (EOC) considers that the burden of proof should be on the employer, as is the case in some other types of dismissal, such as dismissal for trade union activities; it should not be on the employee.

Contractual rights

A woman's experience of employment during pregnancy is often influenced as much by the implied terms and conditions of her employment contract as it is by the expressed terms. It is not easy to assess the number of potential beneficiaries of the provision relating to maintenance of contractual rights during maternity leave, since a lot will depend on how generously this provision is interpreted and on how strictly it is enforced. At present in the UK approximately a third of employers suspend a woman's contract of employment during the unpaid portion of maternity leave, so automatically suspending any contractual rights and benefits, for example:

- over 50 per cent exclude the period of maternity leave for pension purposes;
- over 60 per cent exclude it for holiday entitlements.

The former becomes especially problematic when an employer or female employee is concerned with pension entitlements, since often full entitlement is linked to periods of continuous undisrupted service which, given the low level of childcare provision and lack of paternity leave, many women are unlikely to have achieved for sections of their paid working life.

If, however, this directive's proposal to maintain all contractual rights during pregnancy is interpreted to mean contractual benefits such as low mortgage interest rates, company cars, pension entitlements, accrual of annual leave, and sick leave, as well as contractual rights, the number of UK gainers is likely to be very high. (It should be noted that a woman absent on maternity leave might be able to claim under domestic and European law that she is entitled to the contractual benefits equivalent to those a man receives for sickness absence.)

Health and safety

The health and safety provisions of the directive will benefit an estimated 8,000 women per annum who currently have to leave their jobs because of unacceptable working conditions, as well as about 1,000 other women who are dismissed each year because no alternative work is available for them. The directive also contains a requirement for employers to assess the nature, degree and duration of exposure to health risks in their workplaces and decide what measures should be taken; employees have to be kept informed about the legal requirements and all improvements or changes introduced to meet them. This will mean that a greater number of pregnant women will have access to safety information than in the past, and will be able to make more informed decisions.

Eligibility for maternity pay

At present all women in the UK, irrespective of their hours of work, are entitled to flat rate Statutory Maternity Pay (SMP) if they have six months' service with the same employer by the fifteenth week before confinement and earn over the national insurance threshold. About 20 per cent of employed pregnant women receive no maternity pay whatsoever. It is possible that this is to due to the earnings requirement and non-take-up rather than the service requirement. At the latest count, almost 2.25 million working women (almost one fifth of all working women) were earning less than the lower earnings limit for national insurance (House of Commons, 1991). It is by no means certain that the directive will reform this situation, since with the abolition of Wages Councils low wage earners have less support and reduced opportunity to secure decent wages.

The provision guaranteeing a payment equivalent to that which the employee would receive if absent from work for health reasons implies that the lower earnings limit threshold criterion would stay in place, since this is also one of the criteria for receipt of statutory sick pay.

Level of maternity pay

Flat rate Statutory Maternity Pay is currently worth £47.95 per week (1993), and is payable for up to 18 weeks. Higher rates, that is, 90 per cent of average earnings, is payable for six weeks to staff with two years' continuous full-time service or for five years' part-time, followed by 12 weeks' flat rate payments. The proposal in the directive to link maternity pay with the pay to which the employee would be entitled in the event of absence for health reasons seems to imply parity with lower rate Statutory Sick Pay (SSP), standard rate SSP, or invalidity pension. It seems unlikely therefore that women in the UK will gain any significant financial benefit from the directive, since the usual sickness benefits are worth only about a quarter of the average full-time female worker's income.

Maternity Provisions of the Trade Union Reform and Employment Rights Bill

The Trade Union Reform and Employment Rights Bill is the most important piece of legislation with respect to equal opportunities in the UK that has been produced for some considerable time. In particular, the clauses and schedules covering employment rights contain a range of proposals which will have a significant impact on equality of opportunity for women and men in employment.

Maternity rights and a safety net on pay are fundamental to the aims of achieving equal opportunities between women and men, and enabling women to reach their full potential in the work-force. Getting the bill right and amending it where appropriate will be a benchmark of the seriousness of the government's intentions to achieve these aims.

One important area of opportunity offered by the bill is that of ensuring consistency with other legislation and so simplifying employment protection legislation for the benefit of employers and employees alike. Many of the bill's provisions represent piecemeal additions to various existing provisions, so making employment protection legislation more complex. Equality legislation and employment policy is an already over-complex issue and the EOC has sought to remedy this in its formal proposals to government in 1988 and 1990.

There is an equally pressing need to consolidate the current hotchpotch of legislative provisions for maternity leave and pay. The EOC considers that the absence of provision for maternity pay is a serious defect of the bill.

Contents and evaluation of potential impact

Duration of maternity leave Clause 20 and Schedule 2 of the bill would give a right to all employees, irrespective of length of service, to at least 14 weeks' maternity leave. This means that an employee with six months' service would be treated the same as an employee with six years' service in respect of her entitlement to maternity leave. The length of service clause has been a notorious obstacle – one peculiar to the UK – to improving the maternity rights of all women, not only those with a certain length of service behind them.

The rights for those who already qualify under the Employment Protection (Consolidation) Act (EP(C)A) for the right to return for up to 29 weeks after childbirth remains intact. The proposal to extend the right to some maternity leave irrespective of length of service is a clear advance. However, British women at present take on average 20 weeks' leave for the birth of their first child, and 18 weeks for subsequent births. It is questionable, as already mentioned, whether many will wish to, or be able to, exercise a right to return after only 14 weeks.

While this pattern is likely to be influenced to an extent by statutory entitlement, other factors, such as the absence here of parental leave and of adequate, affordable childcare provision, are also major factors.

The primary purpose of maternity rights legislation is to safeguard the health and well-being of mothers and babies; it does this in part by allowing a period of leave during which the new mother can be confident that her job is protected. The duration of leave must be of sufficient length if this objective is to be achieved.

Timing of maternity leave Sections 34(1) and (2) of the bill propose that the 14-week maternity leave period should start on the first day on which the employee is absent from work 'wholly or partly because of pregnancy or childbirth'. If the absence begins before the eleventh week before confinement, the maternity leave period would begin that week (i.e. the eleventh week before confinement).

Under the new arrangements it is clear that some women could find themselves forced through pregnancy-related ill health to take up to 11 of their 14 weeks' maternity leave before the birth – more if the birth is delayed – leaving a patently inadequate period of guaranteed leave after the birth.

The proposal extends also to women entitled to the right to return 29 weeks after childbirth. Until now this group have had the right, whatever their state of health, to decide for themselves when to stop work. Women entitled to the right to return 29 weeks after childbirth will, on the other hand, retain the right to postpone their return for up to four weeks on production of a medical certificate. There is no similar provision for women entitled to only 14 weeks' leave.

The effect of all this would be to defeat in some cases the intention of the legislation. Moreover, it has been successfully argued under the Sex Discrimination Act (SDA) that, in relation to recruitment, promotion, leave, access to contractual sick arrangements and dismissal, it can be unlawful to treat a pregnant woman less favourably than a sick man would be treated (the so-called 'comparative approach'). It could well therefore be discriminatory to prevent a woman access to sick leave on the grounds that she is pregnant or recovering from the effects of childbirth.

Maintenance of contractual rights and benefits The new bill provides for the maintenance during maternity leave of 'the benefit of the terms and conditions of employment', with the exception of pay (which is to be dealt with separately). The exclusion of pay in this context results in a lack of clarity about which contractual rights are to be maintained. There is a need to define more clearly the status of non-cash financial benefits forming part of the 'terms and conditions of employment'.

It is worth noting that the directive provides for the maintenance of contractual rights during maternity leave, defined as a period of at least 14 weeks. It can be argued that the maintenance of contractual rights should apply to the entire leave period, whatever its length, to ensure consistency with the directive.

Furthermore, there may also be grounds under the Sex Discrimination Act for a woman to claim that she is entitled during maternity leave to the same contractual benefits as a man would receive if he was absent from work because of sickness.

Suspension on health and safety grounds Clause 22 and Schedule 3 provide an employee who would otherwise have to be suspended from work for designated health and safety reasons with a right to be offered suitable alternative work and, if no such work is available, to be suspended on full pay. Employees who unreasonably refuse to undertake suitable alternative work would not be entitled to be paid during suspension. The directive also provides for the maintenance of contractual rights during such periods of necessary suspension. This appears to have been omitted from the bill.

At present, an estimated 8,500 pregnant women per annum are forced to leave their jobs because of unacceptable working conditions. A further estimated one thousand are dismissed because no alternative work is available. The bill's proposals may therefore represent a welcome advance, though the extent to which women will benefit is not yet clear since the grounds on which they will be entitled to be offered alternative work and suspension will be dealt with in separate legislation.

The bill also does not define 'suitable' alternative work, nor what might constitute an unreasonable refusal to undertake it. It could therefore be interpreted in such a way that women refusing work which attracts, for example, less pay, or has different hours, or takes place in a different location, lose the right pay during suspension.

Protection against dismissal Clause 21 provides for all employees, irrespective of their length of service or hours of work, the right not to be dismissed on the grounds of pregnancy or childbirth. Employees who are dismissed during pregnancy or maternity leave are to be given written reasons for dismissal. The length-of-service qualifying condition in the EP(C)A for protection against selection for redundancy on the grounds of pregnancy or maternity would be removed.

The EOC has long advocated the removal of qualifying conditions for protection against dismissal on the grounds of pregnancy. It therefore welcomes this proposal, as it will offer some protection to the estimated 4,000 pregnant British women who are forced to leave their jobs earlier than intended every year. The biggest gainers will be women working in unskilled and semi-skilled occupations, who are twice as likely as managerial and professional women to experience dismissal.

The bill will not of course eradicate dismissal on the ground of pregnancy. As is shown by the National Association of Citizens Advice Bureaux report, *Not in Labour*, unscrupulous employers often cite spurious reasons for dismissal in an attempt to circumvent the law. This is borne out by the EOC's experience; employers rarely admit openly that pregnancy was the reason for dismissal. It can be very difficult for an employee to prove that the reason for her dismissal is pregnancy related. While the proposal that employers should provide written reasons for dismissal will contribute to a reduction in such difficulties, it should be made clear that in future the burden of proof as to the cause of dismissal during pregnancy will lie with the employer.

Issues not addressed by the bill

It is cause for regret that the bill contains no provisions for paternity and parental leave to facilitate the sharing of childcare responsibilities between women and men, although such leave is widely available in other EU countries. Further, the government has not taken the opportunity offered by this legislation and by the EU Childcare Recommendation to look afresh at statutory provision to enable mothers and fathers effectively to combine paid employment with their family commitments.

In any discussion of maternity rights, it is important to bear in mind the practical restriction of parental choice resulting from the low levels of childcare provision in the UK, since the link between the availability of childcare and women's ability to return to work is well documented.

Some of the concerns outlined above may be beyond the scope of the Employment Bill, but they form an important part of the public debate about the effect of childbearing on equality of opportunity between women and men in the labour market.

There is cause for concern both at the speed with which this legislation is being pushed through Parliament and at the absence of public information about its contents. These factors, combined with a general lack of related publicity, must surely detract from the democratic process. It is very important that ample opportunity should be given to women, their employers and interested organizations to be meaningfully involved in the consultative process. Such consultation would give a better chance of achieving maternity rights legislation which avoids past mistakes, and is basically workable.

There should be a publicity campaign, aimed at both small and large organizations, setting out the employment rights of a woman who becomes pregnant. The maternity provisions of the EP(C)A have attracted a great deal of criticism over the years because of their burdensome complexity. The EOC has consistently urged the government to take the opportunity offered by the directive to review and amend UK maternity rights legislation, with the aim of producing a scheme which is clear, simple and well understood by pregnant women and their employers. The whole procedure must be made more accessible, less harrowing, free and simple to use, perhaps along the lines of the Social Security Appeal Tribunals.

The Equal Opportunities Commission is therefore disappointed by the general approach that has been adopted, i.e. that of adding amendments to the EP(C)A, as a means of implementing the directive. However, the task at hand is to make recommendations for amendments to the present bill with the objective of making it clearer and more effective in the level of protection which it offers.

Options for improvement

- to recommend a period of 18 weeks' maternity leave (to coincide with the statutory maternity pay period) with the preservation of the right to return 29 weeks after childbirth for those who qualify;
- as above, but for a new entitlement to parental leave for all women (and men) to follow on from the 18 weeks' leave (note that the right to return could not be abolished without as good a right being substituted, since the directive allows no derogation of existing rights);
- to recommend a period of maternity leave of 29 weeks for all employed pregnant women, irrespective of length of service or hours of work;
- that sections 34(1) and (2) of the bill be removed, so that the right to decide when to start taking maternity leave is left entirely with the employee, in line with current arrangements;
- that all women, irrespective of length of service, are given the right to delay their return from maternity leave in the event of sickness on production of a medical certificate;
- to recommend that the bill clarifies what non-cash benefits or rights will be maintained through the 14-week period, for example, holiday entitlements, pension rights, and usual terms and conditions of employment;
- to recommend that the bill is amended to specify that all contractual terms and conditions except pay but including non-cash financial benefits are maintained throughout the whole period a woman is absent because of maternity.
- to recommend that the bill makes the following provisions:
  (a) for the maintenance of contractual rights during periods of suspension, as required by the directive;

(b) a definition of 'suitable' which makes it clear that alternative work must not involve less favourable conditions, including those relating to remuneration;
(c) that there should be a presumption in law that a dismissal during pregnancy or maternity leave is on the grounds of pregnancy or childbirth, rebuttable by the employer.

According to the Equal Opportunities Commission, between 1989 and 1991 pregnancy-related complaints increased threefold. The big problem is the difficulty of enforcing the legal rights that exist on paper. These are regularly infringed, and discrimination during pregnancy and maternity leave is one of the largest and fastest-growing areas of enquiry for the Equal Opportunities Commission. It is during maternity that many women experience direct discrimination for the first time. Many women are either dismissed or lose benefits, are passed over for promotion or subjected to less favourable terms during this period. There are many reports from Citizens' Advice Bureaux and individuals of employers reacting unfavourably when a woman employee announces her pregnancy. In addition, many employers are unsure of those rights which are provided by law to an employee in this situation; this often results in confusion and the employer treading so carefully that it sometimes breeds resentment.

Just what are an employee's rights and obligations in these circumstances? What are the provisions which an employer should be aware of when an employee says she is pregnant? Pregnancy-related employment rights fall, conveniently, into two categories:

1 employment protection rights;
2 non-discrimination rights, under the Sex Discrimination Act and European law.

Employment protection rights

A number of basic rights are provided by the Employment Protection (Consolidation) Act 1978, referred to as the EPCA, and associated provisions. These should be regarded as the female employee's minimum entitlement and it is quite acceptable for any employing organization to provide better rights than those set out in the EPCA; indeed this has been expressly provided for in this Act, especially with regard to the right to maternity leave, which we will examine further. Four basic provisions are outlined in the EPCA:

(1) Statutory maternity pay The rights to maternity pay are actually set out in regulations known as the Statutory Maternity Pay (General) Regulations (S.I. 1986 No 1960). There is, first, the right to receive a minimum payment during the period of leave, for a limited period. The right depends on the individual's period of employment prior to her actual date of confinement, or the expected birth.

To qualify for statutory maternity pay the employee must satisfy three conditions. She must:

1 have been on a contract which continued until the fifteenth week before the week when the baby is due; this does not require the employee to have been 'at work' but to have been employed at that date. For example, she may have been absent owing to illness, but at that time her contract would have been continuing;
2 also have been continuously employed for 26 weeks. The definition of continuous employment is quite technical and is outlined in the EPCA. Essentially there must not have been a break in the employment, when the contract of employment was not in existence;
3 earn £53.99 or more per week.

Having satisfied these provisos, the employee is entitled to receive maternity pay for 18 weeks. The amount of maternity pay varies, depending on the employee's length of employment. If she has been employed for two years or more, then she will receive higher rate SMP, at 90 per cent of her normal weekly earnings for the first six weeks, and lower rate SMP (currently £44.50) for a further 12 weeks.

Offsetting payments: Where two years' employment has not been achieved, but the employee can satisfy the 26-week test, then lower-rate SMP will be paid for the entire 18 weeks.

Any employer is free to agree to pay more than the statutory payments. But the SMP payments laid down in the Act, which are made, can be offset against the employer's National Insurance contributions.

(2) Antenatal appointments The second main right given is to have reasonable time off work to attend antenatal appointments. The right is to paid time off. To exercise the right the fact of the appointment must be established, and this will avoid the right being abused. The individual must show that she has an appointment at a clinic or other similar establishment at the recommendation of her doctor.

The right itself is limited to reasonable time off. If an employer requires an individual to work additional hours to make up for the time taken to attend antenatal appointments he or she will be in breach of legal provisions, as this will be denying the individual her rights.

(3) Right to maternity leave or the right to return to work The most controversial right, and that which often causes both the employer and employee most concern, is the right to maternity leave. It is really the right to return to work after birth. The EPCA sets out strict legal obligations on the employee to issue notices and comply with time limits. In summary, these requirements are as follows:

- to give 21 days' notice of intended absence;
- to return to work within 29 weeks;
- to give 21 days' notice of intention to return.

These time limits are very strictly construed. An individual who fails to comply with them by missing a time limit or failing to give a particular notice will automatically lose her right to return.

To qualify for her right to return an employee must have been employed for two years in full-time employment (16 hours or more per week) or for five years as a part-time employee (between 8 and 16 hours per week). In addition she must also be working under a contract of employment immediately before the eleventh week before expected confinement.

The employer is entitled to request a medical certificate confirming the expected week of confinement, so that he or she knows what to expect.

Before an individual can exercise her right to return, she must comply with all the notice requirements. She must inform her employer, in writing, at least 21 days before her absence begins, or as soon as reasonably practicable thereafter:

- that she is due to be absent because she is pregnant;
- that she intends to return to work; and
- the date of the expected week of confinement.

Sometimes female employees are dismissed just before their second anniversary of employment, to deprive them of their right to return to work. Employers should be extremely careful to have a good and justifiable reason, if an individual is to be dismissed without notice.

Having ensured that the current notice of departure is given, an individual has further obligations. The employee must return at any time up to 29 weeks after the week of the actual birth (the actual date of confinement), giving 21 days' notice before returning. The 29-week period can be extended to 40 weeks, if there are medical problems following the birth, but the employer must first be notified. The employer can also ask for written confirmation of intention to return, seven weeks after the birth.

The right is to be allowed to return to the same job which the woman was doing prior to her departure, if this is reasonably practicable. Where this does not prove possible, suitable alternative employment must be offered.

Only a small employer is given an exception to these provisions. A small employer is one with five or fewer employees, who can be excused only if it can be shown that it is not reasonably practicable for the employee to return or to be offered alternative employment.

(4) Strengthened unfair dismissal rights Finally, an individual with two years' full-time or five years' part-time employment has the right not to be dismissed by reason of her pregnancy. The phrase used in the legislation is 'dismissed for pregnancy or any other reason connected with pregnancy'. The right covers not just the fact of the pregnancy, but any reason with some connection to it. It may therefore also include miscarriage. This can cause obvious problems, more particularly where a woman's pregnancy-related absence leads an employer to want to dismiss her.

If an employee is dismissed because of her pregnancy or reason connected with it, then that dismissal will be automatically unfair. An employer's only defence is to show that, at the time of the dismissal, the individual was incapable of doing the work which she was employed to do, or that, as an employer, he or she would have been contravening an enactment or a statutory duty in allowing her to continue. This therefore is a test which any industrial tribunal must apply, when considering any complaint brought before it under these provisions. However, the test does not end there; the employer must offer suitable alternative employment or establish that none was available.

Sex discrimination rights

An individual may claim that her dismissal or her mistreatment because of her pregnancy was discrimination, i.e. that she was treated less favourably because of her sex. The European Court of Justice (ECJ) has also formed the view that, if the employer treats an employee less favourably, because of the pregnancy and against provisions governed by the EU's Equal Treatment Directive (which reflects the sex discrimination provisions outlined above in England and Wales), that is discrimination.

The ECJ is of the view that there is no need to assess how a male employee would have been treated. The fact that the pregnancy was the reason behind the decision means it was a sex-based decision and is therefore discrimination. In England and Wales, the tribunals, and indeed the Court of Appeal, have taken a different view: the test here is whether the female employee has been treated less favourably than a man. In order to apply this test, the court asks how an employer would have treated a male employee. This is not an easy question to ask given that men do not get pregnant! So the courts will consider how a man in comparable circumstances would have been treated, for example, a man who is likely to be absent owing to illness for the same length of time.

In October 1992, EU member states accepted the terms of a pregnancy directive. This means that all twelve member states will, within two years, introduce the following protection for pregnant employees:

- protection against substances and processes which could endanger their health and restrictions on night working, on the advice of an individual's doctor;
- a right to paid time off for antenatal examinations;
- minimum 14 weeks' maternity leave to all, regardless of length of service;
- protection against dismissal, regardless of length of service;
- protection against minimum pay and an obligation on all employers to assess risks and adjust working conditions to protect pregnant employees;
- a right to retain all contractual rights during the maternity leave.

For some countries these changes will be quite radical. In England and Wales this will afford greater protection to pregnant employees than that currently in existence. Employers will have to be much more careful in their dealings and treatment of pregnant employees in the future.

Finally, what of the fathers? Recent legislation proposed by Parliament would allow parents to have up to three-months away from work after the baby's birth. How the three-months period is divided and which parents and close relatives may claim this time off will be seen if or when progress on the Employment Protection (Parental Leave) Bill is made. The trend seems to be in favour of rights not just in motherhood, but in parenthood also.

3

Eurostructural Funds and Childcare

There are three European structural funds: the European Regional Development Fund (ERDF), the European Social Fund (ESF), and the European Agricultural Guidance and Guarantee Fund (EAGFF). (In 1988 the funding system was reformed in order to ensure that the closer integration of member states resulting from the Single European Act was accompanied by balanced social and economic development. Their objectives have been clarified and prioritized, giving more assistance to less developed regions and improving co-ordination of the funds at regional level. Discussions and lobbying are under way to determine the regions to be designated for Objectives 1, 2 and 5b of the structural funds. Although the final decisions in respect of funds and their allocation are based largely on economic criteria it is inevitable that there will be some borderline cases where political pressure could tip the balance.) A major event at the beginning of 1993 was the publication of the European Commission's policy document on the 1994–9 structural fund programme.

The key points to note about all three funds are:

1 Merseyside, the Highlands and Islands, Hainault (Belgium) and Cantabria (Spain) have been proposed for Objective 1 status, with Abruzzo (Italy) losing out.
2 The present Objectives 3 and 4 will be integrated into a new Objective 3, combating long-term unemployment and facilitating the integration of young people and the socially excluded into working life.

  The new Objective 4 is aimed at facilitating the adaptation of workers to industrial change. The change is of major significance in that it will reopen the possibilities of using the ESF for the retraining of employed workers.

3 The planning cycle will be simplified and made more 'transparent', with the draft plans and programmes being submitted simultaneously, possibly in the form of a single document.
4 The concept of EU initiatives will be continued more or less unchanged, except that a more flexible approach will be adopted over support for 'ineligible' areas.
5 The activities which Objective 1 funding may support will be broadened to include education and health.

The Funds' Objectives

The funds have five major objectives:

1 promoting the development and structural adjustment of less developed regions;
2 converting the regions seriously affected by industrial decline;
3 combating long-term unemployment;
4 encouraging the integration of young people into employment;
5 (a) speeding up the adjustment of agricultural structures and (b) promoting the development of rural areas.

Eligibility for Union finance

There is a considerable amount of misinformation about the availability of EU finance. It is not easy to summarize the wealth of information, loans, grants and schemes but the following principles should be borne in mind at least:

- The project should generally fall within the scope of a Treaty objective.
- Funds are not made available to support projects which fall within the scope of state aids. It is for this reason that, in general, Union grants are not directly awarded to support capital investment by the private sector or research and development activity involving partners from only one country, or vocational training initiatives with no transnational aspects.
- Over the years there has been a continuous trend towards the administration of EU funds at national and even local level. This is a further manifestation of the subsidiarity principle. Potential applicants are often served best by collecting as much information as possible from local sources before they submit their application forms. One effect of this trend is that, to a degree, EU money is being spent in different ways throughout the Union. Furthermore, from the standpoint of potential

applicants, national officials are becoming more important than their Union counterparts.

How childcare fits in

Work carried out for the European Commission by the Commission's Childcare Network established that inadequacies in childcare contribute to a number of significant structural inequalities within the European Union. Inadequate childcare:

- affects women's access to employment, education and training;
- affects women's hours of work and nature of employment;
- reinforces gender divisions in labour through assumptions about male and female work;
- contributes to skill shortages;
- increases employers' recruitment and training costs.

In those countries in which policies emphasize responsibility either of parents themselves or employers for making childcare arrangements, this can contribute to a widening gap in infrastructure between areas.

Childcare and economic development

The development of childcare facilities can assist and stimulate economic development:

- through removing barriers to the effective use of the potential labour force;
- through facilitating entry to training in areas of required skills.

Quantitatively this can be of significance in offsetting labour market reductions. Qualitatively, it can assist in developing particular skills or addressing the absence of certain skills in the local labour force. The development of childcare facilities is directly relevant to the economic concerns contained within the objectives of the European structural funds.

Childcare conditions attached to funds

Since October 1989 a new clause has been introduced to Union Support frameworks. This stipulates:

> The actions and measures taken in the framework of this Union Support framework must conform with and, where appropriate con-

tribute to the impact of Union policy and legislation relating to equality of opportunity between women and men. In particular, consideration must be given to training and infrastructure requirements which facilitate labour force participation by people with children.

The distribution of funds

The management of the allocation of funds is through partnerships at local, national, regional and Community level. Member states submit development plans setting out their proposals for achieving the five objectives of the fund, complemented by more detailed operational programmes. These indicate the measures to resolve specific employment problems and have to demonstrate clear links with plans and priority activities set out in the Union's support frameworks. All individual projects have to form part of an operational programme.

Other sources of funding

As well as European funding most EU member states have other sources of funding, both in the public and private sector, which can assist special initiatives in the field of education, training and employment promotion. Although there is clearly significant national variation in the application and distribution of funding, there is often as much regional and local variation also. For this reason interested individuals or groups should always check funding regulations and procedures locally first. Some sources of funding which may be available to assist organizations or individuals implement family policies include:

- funding under a positive action programme;
- funding for special provision for people with disabilities;
- ethnic minority grants from government departments;
- out-of-school childcare grants;
- enterprise grants for business start-up programmes;
- grants for women entrepreneurs interested in self-employment such as Local Enterprise Initiatives (LEIs);
- lone parents childcare support grants to enable lone parents to seek education and employment in a 'flexible training hours' environment.

To find out more about what might be available in local areas the following organizations might be worth contacting:

- local libraries;
- Chambers of Commerce;
- European Information Centres;
- disability rights groups;
- race equality centres;
- women's groups;
- citizens' advice centres;
- training organizations, e.g. in the UK the local Training and Enterprise Council (TEC), or Local Enterprise Companies (LECs).

The European Social Fund

The ESF aims to combat unemployment and encourage the regeneration of areas in decline, through (*inter alia*) financial support for vocational training and employment measures. In Britain, it has been seen as a particularly important source because of the relative lack of public funding explicitly targeted at women, ethnic minorities, and disadvantaged groups. The measures under Objective 3 and 4 of the structural funds, for example, allow funds to be allocated for women-only training. They target women wanting to re-enter the labour market after a long absence and unemployed women wanting training in occupations in which women are underrepresented. Funds are also available for childcare provision. In addition, the ESF funds the New Opportunities for Women (NOW) initiative which aims to combat problems of equal opportunities in employment and vocational training by providing funding for transnational women's activities.

The ESF is likely to become an even more important source of funding for training organizations in particular, and for other organizations that offer positive action programmes for women returners. Obtaining ESF funding requires that organizations invest quite substantial resources in the effort. EC procedures have become more user-friendly over the years, but remain enormously complex, bureaucratic and time-consuming. There are, however, economies of scale, and this is one area in which networking at a regional level, both to share expertise and to prepare joint bids, may prove an effective strategy.

It should, however, be noted that one such problem apparently arising through ESF-funded training is that providers and their trainees have experienced increasing problems with the welfare benefit system. In order to ensure that trainees were no worse off as a result of joining their schemes, providers have had to design courses to meet benefit regulations as much as training needs.

Networking in Europe

Networking is the key ingredient of successful partnerships, transnational links and multinational projects and campaigns. Half the population – men – are used to it. Many men-only organizations provide exclusive access to resources which should be available to all without the subtle sex discrimination that denies access and certain privileges to women: community facilities and resources, sports, jobs, business deals, politics and supposedly 'public' appointments. It is only through the setting up of women's networks that women have gradually started to participate in the formal activities associated with networking, although informal or local manifestations of neighbourly networks have, of course, always been a crucial element of women's communication networks.

Once a group has at least some idea of what it wants to achieve through a partnership its members may like to ask themselves some questions:

- What's on offer and where?
- How much does it cost, if anything?
- Are grants or other forms of financial help available?
- How do we go about forming a partnership or increasing the strength of our network?
- Is it the right or best thing for our group?
- Have we any plans for expansion?

The addition of a European section in almost all organizations could not have come at a more important time. Debates on the single market, monetary union, the Social Chapter, the European Union's responsibility towards the former Yugoslavia, eastern Europe, parts of crisis-torn Africa, have all been largely male-dominated and all but ignored those who make up more than half the population of Europe: women.

Even the EU decision to introduce a minimum maternity leave of 14 weeks and the childcare recommendation were, to all intents and purposes, taken by men. Small wonder there are times when the mere mention of Europe makes women feel excluded. Yet women must recognize the opportunities that Europe presents, draw encouragement from its strengths and reduce its inequalities. Through partnerships and transnational projects important links can be forged that can, if the will remains strong, be unbreakable.

All the major issues that affect women's lives will increasingly be enacted on the wider European stage. Women's networks already exist throughout Europe to publicize the campaigns to increase childcare provision, maternity and paternity rights, and equality of opportunity between men and women. Links like these must grow so that women everywhere in Europe can rely on each other for information on what can be done to build equality. Comparative statistics can tell us a great deal, but exchanging the practical experience of women themselves is essential if we are to be able to make any meaningful comparisons between systems of childcare, parental leave, employment rights, maternity rights, health matters and state benefits. Until all of them are improved the list of potential gains has no end. It is only by examining and being aware of provisions which affect employees in other member states that we become entirely sure of where we stand. The EU directive on minimum maternity leave for women in employment is a good case in point. UK opposition to the original proposal to guarantee working women 14 weeks on full pay was the driving force in the 'compromise' to reduce payment to the level of sick pay in each of the member states. Even with this watered-down provision the UK based Maternity Alliance estimates that 200,000 women a year will benefit in this country, widely agreed to have the poorest maternity provision in the EU. The UK is the only country in the EU where maternity leave is not a universal right for employed women. To qualify, women must have worked for the same employer for two years if working full time, five if working part time. This rule means that overall an estimated 40 per cent of employed women fail to qualify, with two out of every three part-time women workers excluded from statutory provision. If this looks bleak in comparison with other EU countries, the picture looks even bleaker when compared to the rest of Europe. Provision for maternity, paternity and parental leave in eastern Europe and in Scandinavia moves the European average up several significant notches.

It's not just in looking at provision for parental leave and childcare – another area where this country lags badly behind – that we can hope to benefit from an active exchange of information and experiences with women throughout the whole of Europe. We could look as well at the French legislation which says that perpetrators of sexual harassment face up to one year in gaol and fines of up to 100,000 francs; or examine the extension of career breaks in Belgium to include other personal and family reasons besides childbirth, and argue that it should apply universally; and look to private sector employees who currently depend on individual agreements, as well as to public sector workers who have guaranteed rights.

Women in Europe can also raise questions about their share in power and how that can affect their progress towards real equality. Belgium has had compulsory positive action programmes for women in the public sector since 1990, and similar voluntary programmes in the private sector are backed with government grants and practical assistance. In recent years both Italy and the Netherlands have introduced national laws which back positive action programmes with legal and financial incentives. In France all private sector employers must submit a report on the position of their women employees which has to include an 'equality action plan' to enable women to catch up.

If strong links are established between different groups and projects now, individuals and organizations will be better prepared to meet head-on the 'new' issues that are set to emerge in the coming years. Political and economic changes coupled with the changes we all face throughout Europe as a result of an ageing population suggest that we would do well to equip ourselves now with the transnational know-how generated through networking and partnerships. Whatever we can learn by comparing legislative systems which point to major differences in women's rights, we are constantly reminded of the essential sameness of women's lives, in that they are the major providers of skilled work in the home. The message that emerges from countries where women's participation in employment is high is of women utterly exhausted by their dual role as full-time earner and main family worker. This double burden that women carry means that a progressive number system of legislation which encourages women into employment on the same basis as men is not, on its own, enough to achieve equality. The rules of the employment game, drawn up in the male dominated boardrooms were designed from a male perspective, which hardly surprisingly caters more for men's needs than women's needs. Granting parents equal shares in parental leave, for example, means little choice for a couple with big differences in earnings and career potential. Until men can take an equal share in the work of childcare and home life without financial or employment prejudice to either partner, they will not do it and women will be scorned for expecting them to. Much greater changes in the system are needed.

Networking methods are:

- among universities or institutions of education;
- commercial and academic partnership, e.g. between universities and industry;
- partnerships between women's groups;
- partnerships between women in industry;
- occupational partnerships, for example, between female teachers, engineers, local government personnel.

They may be assisted by:

- EU grants;
- EU programmes;
- independent transnational research bodies, for example, CREW (Centre for Research into European Women); CREW has developed a wide experience in European business and training partnerships;
- colleges and universities;
- industry;
- trade unions;
- women's organizations;
- voluntary organizations.

Networking gives the following benefits:

- There is a venue for action and therefore for discerning shortcomings, implementing knowledge and expertise, developing new skills and measuring the capacity to achieve results.
- There is a venue for professional and social commitment where contacts with other people are subject to the constraints of reality and production.
- It assists individuals to gain meaning from their own working practices, particularly when the common problems which underlie them are shared, analyzed and perceived.

Dissemination of good practice

An obvious side-effect of the creation of twelve independent EU member states, working to a common framework, but with national leadership and locally determined objectives, is that there will be a lot of variety, but a lot of duplication also. Many organizations will make the same mistakes, and many will not hear of the solutions which others have found. It is rapidly becoming a cliché that just as research reports always conclude with a call for further research, so discussions of transnational policies in any specific areas end with a call for better networking to share and disseminate good practice.

The parental rights and childcare areas are no exception. There are factors which militate strongly in favour of such networking (e.g. economies of scale in seeking European funding), and some which militate against (e.g. a somewhat competitive environment in some areas may encourage some organizations to keep their good ideas to themselves). It seems, however, that there already exists extensive networking on many issues within local and regional industries. It is clear that these networks perform a valuable function, although one that is often tactical and short term rather than strategic and long term, with emphasis on the sharing of information on specific initiatives, but less on larger strategic issues.

The time may, therefore, be right to build on the work of these more fragmented networks, through the creation of a network or grouping conference (perhaps under the auspices of industry-led bodies) which would tackle the issues of strategy, organization, design, monitoring and funding structures at a higher level.

4

Developing Organizational Policies: Pregnancy and Maternity, Parental Rights and Childcare

Childcare provision has been firmly placed on the economic and political agendas of EU member states for the 1990s. One of the reasons for this is the growing recognition of the multi-functional nature of childcare provision. Not only does it have a labour market related to demographic trends and skills shortages, but also an educational function with the increasing importance attached to pre-school education and environmental factors. Childcare provision also has a welfare function in relation to children with special needs. Integral to these functions is the equal opportunities implications of any childcare provision.

In the face of growing demand and increasing pressure many organizations are looking at innovative ways of providing childcare. However, given the dire financial situation in many enterprises cost-effectiveness is a priority concern.

One scheme that is very promising is the provision of facilities in partnerships involving local authorities, private sector employees, voluntary organizations, educational institutions and other organizations. Working in partnership, a central body can create consortia to fund developments which would otherwise be uneconomic. The local population could benefit, since some places are reserved for community use. These types of partnerships also have the advantage of being a good model for using European structural funds.

Why Childcare?

Demographic changes mean that companies need to attract women responsible for childcare back to work during the 1990s.

There are several ways of doing this:

Flexible working By allowing staff to work 'flexi-time', the company enables them to combine childcare with work.

Job-share Two employees can share one job and childcare too, or make their own part-time childcare arrangements.

Term-time only contracts These allow parents with school-aged children to work full time, but only in term time.

Career break schemes Women who take maternity leave may return to their job or one at the same level at any time within the limits of the 'career break' (usually 3–5 years)

Childcare assistance This can take the form of providing a workplace nursery, holiday play-scheme, after-school club, or allowances to help with the costs. Other assistance could take the form of:

- childcare allowances: a flat-rate contribution to childcare costs payable by the company to parents;
- childcare vouchers, such as those introduced by Luncheon Vouchers, which can only be exchanged for childcare;
- childcare cheques: a scheme developed by William M. Mercer which includes a commission for development work. The cheques are only redeemable by childminders who have been approved by the National Childminding Association, or out-of-school schemes approved by the National Out of School Alliance.

The Advantages to Employers

Recruitment Childcare and 'parent-friendly' working practices attract staff.

Retention Women are more likely to return to work after maternity leave if help with childcare is offered.

Equal opportunities Assistance with childcare encourages equality of access to all employment opportunities.

Company image Flexible working practices and help with childcare are essential for a caring company.

Cost effectiveness The Midland Bank estimates that it loses £17,000 in recruitment, training, and management costs for every employee who does not return after maternity leave. It has now embarked on a programme of 300 nurseries for staff, and finds that its average subsidy of £1,700 per child per year produces real value for money.

Up to now the role of local authorities in most EU member states in children's day care has been to provide a limited safety net of good quality care for a small number of high priority children and a regulatory service for private and voluntary sector schemes and childminders. Many local authorities have had higher ambitions but few have had the resources to do much more. Through the use of partnership schemes the resources that local authorities do have can be used effectively.

Local authorities have a unique range of experience in childcare, covering workplace crèches, day nurseries, after-school clubs, play centres and childminders, which is a substantial resource in itself. Local authorities also have physical assets to offer; schools can be used for after-school clubs and holiday schemes and other land and buildings may also be available. The benefits of partnership nurseries for employers include:

- sharing of costs, especially for small organizations;
- protection from fluctuations in the workforce;
- involvement of local authority and hence its expertise and resources;
- increase in access to education and training for workers;
- enhanced level and quality of labour supply.

The benefits of partnership nurseries for local authorities include:

- rationalization in provision and effective use of existing resources;
- the serving of wider community needs;
- provision for employees;
- the statutory duty towards children in need met in an integrated, unstigmatizing way;
- improvement in labour supply which affects economic development;
- access to training for employees and the local community.

In many parts of the EU the regional or local council and private sector employers together provide not only nurseries, but a wide range of other services including a consultancy service, child-minders, care in the home, crèches, after-school clubs and holiday play-schemes, information, advice and support. In the UK, the American Express company, which has its home in the seaside resort of Brighton, has been able to work successfully with the local council in developing its childcare link scheme.

While ideally childcare provision ought to be community based, as workplaces begin to make their own arrangements for childcare some of the worst problems related to lack of these facilities are overcome. Besides, such partnership schemes do not have to be restricted to the provision of nurseries alone.

The scope for successful intervention is growing. In changing their emphasis from pure regulation to enabling, councils have the opportunity to take a lead in promoting the development of childcare. All authorities should be re-examining their policies with a view to taking full advantage of the potential of partnership schemes in childcare.

Issues for Small and Medium-sized Businesses

Small and medium-sized businesses have the same need as large organizations for a better educated and more flexible workforce. They face the same challenge of remaining adaptable and competitive in an ever-changing business environment.

Some of the initiatives outlined here could be introduced into smaller companies with relatively little modification. Those with a broader scope and more ambitious aims may at first sight seem impossible luxuries for smaller companies with scarce resources. However, there are ways in which these companies can become involved.

A range of opportunities exists for joint ventures among local businesses and other key players in the community. There are already several examples of 'networks' involving smaller companies and education providers and encouraging a social and psychological mix between different generations. In 1990 a new organization called Entr-ages was introduced into Belgium. Initially the stated aim of the network was twofold. The first was to break down the psychological and social isolation of many elderly people in residential care; in order to achieve this, residential homes have been opened up to local people of all ages to encourage a social and intergenerational mix. Its second aim was to increase awareness among the different generations about age-related issues. In the UK, Training and Enterprise Councils (TECs) can play an important role in the creation of such initiatives by acting as 'brokers', helping to link small businesses with local education and training providers and childcare services or with larger companies with established schemes.

It seems that a number of large companies extend their initiatives to local suppliers or to smaller firms more generally. As a result, local communities as a whole are able to benefit from childcare initiatives. A similar approach to partnerships – networking and sharing resources – has also been successful within larger multi-site companies where there are difficulties in resourcing and managing initiatives at smaller sites or single-occupancy sites.

By becoming involved in collaborative ventures, smaller businesses can help their employees – and themselves – to benefit from childcare initiatives. The costs need not be prohibitive. The most important ingredients of success are motivation and commitment.

The Role of Training

We know today that the survival of many firms very much depends on the quality of the continuing training of managers and their employees. In the future, appropriate importance must therefore be attached by decision-makers in senior management and by corporate strategies to continuing training in specific and general subjects. This will be a particular challenge for small and medium-sized firms, since they account for the majority of jobs and also react more quickly to changes in market conditions than large firms. Continuing training has already become a new and growing investment factor. This change is the result, not only of rapid technological development, which constantly poses fresh challenges for employees in almost every sector, but of the increasingly changing image of the work-force, which necessitates changes in management and communication structures in the daily routine of firms.

Several evolutions have had an impact on training in the past decade. Technological evolutions, social and political changes and the internationalization of markets are rendering organizational management and planning increasingly difficult. Change and evolution go hand in hand with uncertainty, the inability to plan, and unpredictability. Where training was mainly an exclusive answer to change, it is now increasingly used to guide the process(es) of change, to monitor change and to prepare people for continuous evolution.

The introduction of family-friendly policies, career break schemes, job sharing, after-school clubs, or whatever other methods organizations are adopting to become more flexible and more responsive to their human resource functions, require attention to be paid to a number of key focal areas including:

- in-company training as part of a future-orientated corporate philosophy and corporate identity;
- in-company training as part of comprehensive investment planning for the future of the firm;
- in-company training as a concept and means of employee development or of the firm's personnel development planning, with particular reference to junior managers at all levels;
- development of objectives of in-company training specific to the firm, and development of concepts related to situations and linked to learning places;
- development of future-orientated qualification profiles specific to each firm for all management tasks;
- development of acceptance strategies for all in-company training activities;
- development of a comprehensive evaluation concept specific to a firm from the angle of 'training control'.

This outline of in-company training tasks reveals that in-company and management training methods must be interdisciplinary, specific and general in design. Macro- and micro-economic, philosophical, psychological and sociological approaches must be linked scientifically and pragmatically to the complex technical and vocational requirements to be met by the players in the practical environment of the firm.

The concept of new in-company and management training methods which focus on family policies are a means of survival in an increasingly competitive economic climate.

- Ensuring the long-term competitiveness of a firm increasingly depends on the qualifications of its employees. Investment in a firm's 'human capital' therefore forms part of the corporate strategy.

- Personnel planning and personnel development or, better, employer and employee development must be systematically linked to in-company training tasks.
- As a rule, investment in training, i.e. investment in a firm's 'human capital' is a long-term investment.
- Investment in training is generally only of benefit in the long term, and its effects cannot be accurately measured. Financial managers are therefore in constant danger of neglecting the need for investment in in-company training.
- The importance of long-term investment in training must have implications for the 'image' and hierarchical position of initial and continuing training in a firm's organizational structure.
- The successful implementation of family-orientated training concepts in a firm's internal structure is greatly facilitated if the training sphere is able to interact with the corresponding practical spheres on at least an equal basis.
- Provided that a firm's 'personnel management' is a central division represented on the management board, the training sphere could be made part of personnel management as a comprehensive 'personnel development sphere'. Otherwise training should be a separate management responsibility. This organizational structure results from the considerable importance that is even now recognizably attached to increasing investment in 'human capital'.
- From this hierarchical position, in-company trainers can tackle their main task of ensuring that the firm has adequately trained employees in the right place at the right time.
- The bitter experience of recent decades with short-term training concepts geared to isolated areas of activity has made it clear that employees must be seen not as 'damage-prone cases in need of repair', but as living beings capable of development with individual features and extensive needs that should not be underestimated.
- Only with training measures can we create an environment in which employees continue to develop their intellectual, personal, individual potential to the best of their ability. No barriers should be put in the way of individuals reaching their potential.
- In-company training concepts, in-company future-orientated initial and continuing training scenarios geared to long-term economic gain must be based on a comprehensive image of people, a management philosophy specific to a firm and a management identity developing on this philosophy. From this it follows, firstly, that the continuing training of employees, for example, cannot be promoted solely by isolated three-day seminars run by external trainers at hotels with sports facilities. Secondly, we depend on highly qualified in-company and management trainers with

developed personalities who are familiar with the particular interests of the firm from many years of experience and who have also undergone high-level further training in in-company and management training methods.
- The in-company and management trainer must be an 'organization developer' if he or she is able to reconcile the firm's economic interests with working conditions that encourage motivation and creativity.
- The in-company and management trainer is the 'presenter' of internal processes aimed at the further development of a management philosophy and corporate identity. Within this intellectual framework, people have an opportunity to further develop their individual potential, which is also to the advantage of the firm concerned.

The EU Childcare Recommendation

In 1992 EU ministers adopted a recommendation urging more action on childcare, recognizing that a serious lack of such provision was a 'major barrier' to women's access and participation in the labour market. The final document is a far cry from the request for a childcare directive, which would be binding on member states, and has been repeatedly urged by the European Parliament. The recommendation outlines instead a voluntary action plan which will depend on private, public, individual or collective initiative. The European Parliament has asked on several occasions for a directive that includes annual childcare targets to bridge the gap between the number of childcare places available and the increasing demand throughout the EU.

The recommendation urges member states to establish or promote childcare initiatives in four areas:

- the provision of childcare services for working parents, parents who are in education or training with a view to employment and those seeking work;
- special leave arrangements for working parents with children;
- the promotion of an 'environment, structure and organization of work to make them more responsive' to the needs of workers with children;
- a more equal sharing of 'occupational family and upbringing responsibilities arising from the care of children' between men and women.

Childcare services are defined in the recommendation as 'any type of childcare, whether public or private, individual or collective'. The role of 'national, regional and local authorities, management and labour, other relevant organizations and private individuals' is repeatedly stressed throughout, as well as the importance of financial contributions by these bodies.

The recommendation states that the role of public authorities in providing childcare in certain member states may be limited, owing to low levels of national income and restricted public spending. It lists five strategies to be encouraged by member states to improve the provision of quality childcare services.

1 These should enable parents who are working, or following an education or training course to obtain employment, or are seeking employment 'to have as much access as possible to local childcare services'. In this context, attempts should be made particularly to ensure that:

- the services are offered at prices affordable to parents;
- they combine reliable care from the point of view of health and safety with a general upbringing and pedagogical approach;
- the needs of parents and children are taken into account when access to services is determined;
- the services are available in all areas and regions of member states, both in urban areas and in rural areas;
- the services are accessible to children with special needs, for example linguistic needs, and to children in lone-parent families, and meet the needs of such children.

2 They should encourage flexibility and diversity of childcare services as part of a strategy to increase choice and meet the different preferences, needs and circumstances of children and their parents while preserving coherence between different services.

3 The training, both initial and continuous, of workers in childcare services should endeavour to be appropriate to the importance of the social and educative value of their work.

4 Childcare services should be encouraged to work closely with parents and with local communities through regular contact and exchanges of information, so as to be responsive to parental needs and particular local circumstances.

5 National, regional or local authorities, management and labour, other relevant organizations and private individuals, should be encouraged in accordance with their respective responsibilities, to make a financial contribution to the creation or operation of coherent childcare services which can be afforded by parents and which offer them a choice.

Member states have agreed that both men and women should be given more flexible leave arrangements to look after their children, and EU ministers have also agreed to take or promote action that could:

- in particular within the framework of collective agreements, create an environment, structure and organization of work which takes into account the needs of all working parents;
- ensure that due recognition is given to persons engaged in childcare services 'as regards the way in which they work and the social value of their work';
- serve as an example in developing initiatives in this area, especially in the public sector.

A greater role for men in childcare was also included in the recommendation. Member states have been asked to encourage 'with due respect for freedom of the individual, the increased participation of men, to achieve a more equal sharing of parental responsibilities between men and women and to enable women to have a more effective role in the labour market'.

Checklist for Action

The maternity and childcare initiatives outlined here raise a variety of issues for a wide range of key players.

Issues for employers

The aims of an initiative What are the company's specific aims? How will the initiative address them?

The constraints Is there a budget? Can resources be pooled with other local employers? Are local providers willing to respond flexibly?

The scope of the initiative What sort of provision will it include? Which employees are to be targeted?

Organization and delivery How should the initiative be organized? Who will manage it? Are there other partners (training or education providers or local companies)? How should various initiatives be delivered? (Remember that suitable methods for services for small children, for instance, may be quite inappropriate for school-age children seeking holiday care or after-school hours care only)

Promotion How can the initiative be publicized to ensure maximum awareness and take-up by employees?

Issues for employer bodies and training organizations

Heightening awareness How can local employers, or employers within a particular sector, be made aware of the benefits of maternity and childcare initiatives?

Encouraging top-level commitment How can the commitment of company leaders be secured?

Facilitating access and co-operation How can large employers be encouraged to open their provision to other local businesses? Can smaller companies be helped by the creation of consortia, partnerships or networks?

Issues for trade unions

Encouraging employer action Can trade unions help to raise awareness of the value of such initiatives?

Encouraging participation What can trade unions do to raise individual awareness of the importance of commitment and motivation to childcare initiatives and family policies in order to secure that continuous improvements are made and funding targets met.

Issues for education providers

Understanding employer aims and employee needs What is the company trying to achieve? What are the particular needs and problems of the students? Are there barriers to access?

Offering advice How can providers help in designing the initiative? What support and counselling can they offer to participant and support providers?

Monitoring

Without effective monitoring an organization cannot be sure if it is achieving its strategic objectives in the organizational policy field. It cannot identify and reward those of its managers and personnel who are making progress, and take remedial action for those who are not;

it cannot promote (and indeed defend) its approach on organizational policy to its local communities.

What is effective monitoring?

The principles involved in effective monitoring of organizational policies are well established and well known. Originally developed for the monitoring of equal opportunities within employing organizations, the principles apply equally with regard to any form of training and staff development programmes, and there is general agreement on the kinds of data which are required as a minimum. The data necessary for effective monitoring are, moreover, the same kinds of data which would be required for normal management information purposes.

Effective monitoring for equal opportunities purposes involves the collection, analysis and feedback of individual level data on staff development programme participants. The data are captured through a regular and systematic process (at a minimum this is likely to be on entry to a training programme, and on exit; but intermediate stages of data capture may also be appropriate, e.g. on submission to a work placement). They are then input to a computerized management information system, which will allow both the production of the kinds of aggregated data required, and the more detailed data necessary to monitor specific activities. Although some organizations may find it is more imperative to concentrate on family policy, for example, the principles and processes are the same with regard to monitoring any equality issue, and any monitoring process would normally aim simultaneously to capture information relating to all forms of equal opportunities target groups.

The elements of monitoring

Key elements of any monitoring system are likely to involve a number of steps:

Data collection at point of entry Firms need to decide for themselves the minimum data set they require. At a minimum, this is likely to include basic data on individuals who participate in family policy working practices such as childcare schemes, holiday playclubs, flexible working arrangements. Ideally the monitoring process would also collect information on applicants who are not accepted for the programme or who choose not to participate in one, which can be crucial information in investigating the causes of any systematic underrepresentation of particular groups on the programme (e.g. is it because these groups do not apply to the programme, perhaps because of inadequate or poorly targeted marketing, or is it that they do apply but are not chosen by the company?).

Data collection at the point of exit from a programme (and intermediate points if appropriate) The monitoring system must be designed so that this information can be linked with the starts information on an individual basis. The ability to undertake tracking at an individual level is crucial for any diagnosis of problems which are revealed at an aggregate level. If this linking is done, then the data set is a 'cohort' rather than two 'cross-sections' and information does not need to be collected on characteristics which will not have changed since entry, or which can be inferred from the entry information (sex, race, date of birth, etc.).

Data analysis At a minimum this will look at entry or participation rates of the different groups on the different programmes, and the relative satisfaction or dissatisfaction of those groups on leaving the programmes (in terms of outcomes, durations, and other performance indicators which an organization is using).

Assessment Having conducted the analysis some baseline or benchmark will be required against which each organization can assess whether performance is 'good' or 'bad'. Normally, for participation rates, this will involve at least a comparison with the representation in the relevant population from which the eligible group is drawn. It is important to get the definition of the relevant group right. For example, the incidence of disability rises with age, as does the need for information about retirement, and it would be inappropriate to compare the proportion of young entrants who are disabled with the proportion of disabled people in the population as a whole. When outcomes are being examined, the comparison will normally be between the various groups participating in the programme (do male participants consistently get better outcomes than female, white participants better than those from ethnic minorities etc.?).

Each organization is likely to set regular targets against which to monitor progress. In the case of participation rates, the targets are likely to be drawn from the representation in the relevant population in question. In the case of outcomes, targets are likely to be set in terms of progress towards equality of outcomes for the different groups.

Feedback and review Finally, the process involves feedback and review of the monitoring assessment with the managers, staff, providers or others responsible for improving performance against the targets. This is an essential part of the managerial process, which will vary from organization to organization; it will, for example, be important to take account of how far failure to achieve targets reflects changes in the external labour market and the organization's inability to influence it. The only general point which can be made is that any effective monitoring system will involve such a feedback and review stage with the key actors involved, on a regular basis.

Monitoring of assessment and guidance processes We have concentrated so far on the monitoring of provision itself, and its outcomes. It is clear, however, that monitoring of the assessment, advice, and guidance procedures is also appropriate, to avoid direct or indirect discrimination on the part of those providing these services; this could result in particular client groups being more likely to be 'directed' to certain types of provision than others.

Sharing systems expertise Few organizations are at the stage of being able to conduct fully effective monitoring of their programmes, and it is understandable, having struggled, and in many cases abandoned the struggle with standard monitoring of equal opportunities issues, that some firms are unenthusiastic at the thought of developing new monitoring systems. Given, however, that some firms are further down the road than others in this respect, there is an important case for sharing existing expertise. It is not inconceivable that some firms would be happy to recoup some of their investment costs in this area, whilst others would be willing to pay to avoid the time and cost involved in 'reinventing the wheel'.

Liaison and networking with other bodies In the childcare field as in the parental rights field there are large numbers of community groups, representative organizations, lobbying bodies and other actors representing or speaking on behalf of members of different organizations.

A key question for co-ordinating bodies and training bodies wishing to make progress on these issues, therefore, is how best they can draw on the expertise and authority of such groups, involve them in decision-making and provision itself. There is no general consensus on this, although there is a clear view in the field that it should be done. Co-ordinating bodies such as the UK-based TECs should:

- have strategic objectives with performance indicators for childcare services, parent-friendly working policies etc., devised in partnership with local childcare support groups;
- have separate subgroups for maternity, paternity rights, childcare etc., so that each issue is treated as an independent issue as well as part of a wider issue;
- be flexible in their consultation strategies;
- be willing to try new approaches based on the advice of local people who have good practice in this field.

It is clear that many co-ordinating bodies such as TECs have set up such groups to deal with childcare and parental issues, and nearly all have community representation of some sort on them. Sometimes there is just one group, and sometimes there are several. No general rules can apply here; much will depend on the size of the TEC and its community, and the number and activity level of the potential community partners.

Beyond these consultation mechanisms, there is a more general question about what kind of liaison, networking, co-ordination or facilitation role the TEC itself can play in the local community. Many TECs and similar organizations in other EU member states need to find ways of acting in a developmental or co-ordination role; providing strategic pump-priming funding where appropriate, and building links between these organizations and some of the mainstream organizations such as employment services, careers advisory services and educational institutions.

In addition, TECs may often be in a key position to act as a bridge between these community networks on the one hand, and employers on the other. Their business-led character gives them the leverage necessary to deal with employers, and it is often argued that employers do not want to liaise with such groups on a fragmented multilateral basis, but would welcome the co-ordinating role to be provided by the TECs, for example.

5

The Advantages to Employers of Flexible Working Patterns: Quality and Equality

Pursuit of quality is now a major priority throughout both the public and private sectors. However, the meaning of quality varies according to the context in which it is used. For example, what quality means within the commercial sector is not necessarily the same as its meaning within the public sector. If this difference is not fully appreciated and addressed, the pursuit of quality can lead to an undermining of organizational goals and values in respect of maternity, childcare and family policies and practices. For many organizations, where people management is valued as highly as profit management, quality is inextricably linked to equity.

Quality through Equality

The idea of quality in employment is necessarily a broad one. The role of most organizations is much wider than simply generating a product for consumption by a certain market sector. It is about being a vehicle for democracy, empowering the citizen, providing accountability, being seen to be fair and establishing principles of equity through ensuring equality of opportunity. Hence, any definition of quality as simply setting standards for a particular service will be totally inadequate for most organizations if it does not incorporate components such as:

- Who is using the service and who is the service not reaching?
- How does this level of uptake relate to those whose needs for it are greatest?
- How diverse is the service in meeting different needs throughout the community?
- How flexible is the service in meeting changes in need?

For quality initiatives that are not based on this wider perception of the concept, success will be elusive regardless of the vigour with which it is pursued. For example, all quality initiatives accept the actual needs of the service user as a primary guiding principle of service provision. However, if it is assumed that the service user is a standard entity with standard needs, the service provided will be suitable for only a small section of the community.

Traditionally the image of the standard consumer has been conceived in terms of a young white man, reflecting the dominant composition of the decision-makers in industry. However, within any community, this sector is likely to be not only the most privileged, but also is likely to be a minority one.

In the UK women make up 54 per cent of the population. It is estimated that well over 10 per cent of the population has a learning or physical disability, and at least 10 per cent of the population is gay or lesbian. The elderly population (over 60s) is currently 21 per cent and projected to rise sharply in the coming years. The black and other ethnic minority population constitute 5 per cent with a concentration of over 50 per cent in some areas. Clearly, it is the large majority of the population that falls into the combined categories of women, black and ethnic minorities, older people, the disabled and lesbians and gay men. It is this large majority who have traditionally not had equal access to services and been inadequately serviced by local communities and their industries in the past.

It is important to dispel the myth that striving for equality of opportunity is about taking on board marginal, minority concerns. Delivering good quality services in the public sector is not really possible without fully addressing diversity of need and equality considerations.

In fact, if equality is not fully integrated into quality, the results obtained could be the opposite of those that are desired. For example, a quality assurance system that does not have inbuilt equality considerations could have the effect of enforcing conformity in meeting set minimum standards rather than actually meeting diverse needs that vary between organizations. Such a system would lead to an erosion rather than enhancement of quality.

Yet too often the emphasis on quality programmes becomes skewed towards visible consumer services such as refuse collection and street cleaning while ignoring the need to establish and improve standards and levels of provision across the whole range of services. This range of services is related to the role of local government as a democratic institution responsible for empowering the citizen. Thus services such as childcare, homelessness advice sessions, meals on wheels provision and community development programmes are just as important a part of local government services as street cleaning or refuse collection, and need to be seen as an integral part of customer care initiatives.

In seeing quality as more than a mechanical exercise of setting standards for existing services the fundamental question, 'Are existing services the most appropriate ones for the population served?' has to be asked. Further, in establishing quality within a climate of financial restraint the issue of resource allocation, and where necessary reallocation, needs to be carefully scrutinized. Where resources are limited, rationing or targeting becomes necessary, with a need to assess disadvantage and prioritize need. In local government, market forces cannot serve this purpose, nor the crude operation of value for money principles that simply take the best to be that which is cheapest.

Equality and Service Delivery

There is ample evidence showing that women, black and minority ethnic people, people with disabilities, older people, lesbians and gay men experience disadvantage in many areas of local community service provision, including housing, education, employment and training, leisure and recreation, and aspects of social service provision. Some of the factors giving rise to this disadvantage include:

- the lack of appropriate services to meet differing needs across the community;
- ignorance or complacency about the nature and level of need;
- lack of investigation of the equalities implications of new proposals and service developments;
- inaccessible nature of services, including place and times of provision, language barriers, as well as physical barriers to access;
- inadequate nature of services, the level of provision being too low to meet even the known level of need;
- poor level of general information on services provided being made available to the public;
- the complex and bureaucratic nature of the procedures used inhibiting service uptake;
- the lack of involvement of community members in the local council's or local organization's decision-making process;

- the lack of a representative workforce within the council or firm that can sensitively reflect and serve the needs of the community;
- the operation of discriminatory practices, which could even be unintentional, amongst those involved in planning, designing and delivering services.

All of the contributory factors giving rise to disadvantage must be addressed and overcome if an authority wants to provide quality services for all. Creating equal opportunities in service delivery may at different times involve:

- identifying undersupply of services (the 'more services approach');
- identifying alternative or new services (the 'different services approach');
- identifying ways of improving existing services (the 'better services approach').

Key Components in Ensuring Quality Services

Equality must be present and central to each department's planning and evaluation process. It should permeate the process of identifying strategic objectives, operational objectives, performance measures and targets. Through understanding the factors that contribute to inequality in service delivery generally, responses to overcome them can be developed as part of a quality initiative. Key components in ensuring good quality service delivery must address the following issues.

Access

Accessibility is a key quality issue, both in terms of physical accessibility and of breaking down social barriers to access. Many organizations have sought to improve access by:

- providing disabled access and clear signposting;
- establishing standards in opening hours, location of facilities and quality of the environment in reception and public areas;
- providing loop systems for employees with hearing impairments;
- providing childcare facilities, e.g. drop-in crèches, play areas or toys distributed in certain key areas;
- sensitizing staff to the varying needs and expectations of the organization's users, including linguistic and cultural differences so as to make initial contacts between staff and consumers more responsive, helpful and friendly.

Responsiveness

For the quality services to be equitable they must be relevant and responsible. Many organizations have addressed this issue by:

- involving the users of services collectively, as well as seeking the views of individuals in the planning and development of services in order to identify new or better ways of delivering services;
- recognizing that the process of canvassing views itself has to be done in such a way as to build up a representative and accurate picture;
- identifying target groups who ought to be using services but are failing to do so, thus revealing gaps in service delivery.

Representation and communication

Service quality can always be improved by ensuring that an organization constantly strives to find out members' needs, views and wishes. The views of members must, therefore, be represented to decision-makers at all levels in the organization. In order to do this many organizations have experimented with:

- wide ranging consultation programmes ensuring that no significant group of actual or potential service users are prevented from representing their views;
- putting all levels within the organisation in touch with, and making them responsive to, the views of the public, which have been gained through consultation exercises as well as through user surveys and exit polls;
- performance management systems which incorporate a range of mechanisms for consumer feedback;
- opening up committee meetings to questions and input from the public;
- developing lines of communication through innovative methods such as encouraging press debate;
- developing customer care initiatives which continually test perceptions of the organization amongst the public and service users.

Information dissemination

People need easy access to basic information about the range of services in a form they can readily understand. Consumers can be empowered, and services made more effective, if information is available about service objectives, standards aimed for and achieved, individual rights and how to complain. Towards this end many organizations have been:

- establishing codes of practice on the way information is provided in relation to what users of services can expect and what they can do if not satisfied;
- disseminating the information widely so that all sections of the community are made aware;
- ensuring that the information provided is easily understood and available in different languages specific to the community.

Redress

Users of services and the public should be able to settle their grievances quickly, easily and fairly. Complaints can be an important source of information about services and the issues raised ought to be fed into the organization's procedures for making policies. In this area some organizations have been:

- establishing and publicizing codes of practice for complaints procedures which clearly specify what remedies or compensations are available and what procedures for appeal exist;
- ensuring that complaints procedures for discrimination, whether existing separately or integrated into the general complaints procedure, are equally well publicized, with remedies including the influencing of organizational changes where necessary;
- establishing mechanisms to ensure that the outcomes of procedures for complaints and redress will also feed into performance management systems.

Managing the delivery of quality services

In order to ensure good quality service delivery, planning for quality has to be fully integrated into an organization's overall service planning and evaluation process. Within this framework the corporate message on quality, including the values embedded within the concept of quality, need to be clearly transmitted to all levels of the organization. It is a basic principle of organizational effectiveness that the members of the organization should have a sense of shared purpose and objectives.

Performance monitoring

Each department, each service and each area of service within an organization should have its own checklist of performance targets explicitly stating what its aims are in the areas of access, responsiveness, communication, information, redress and customer care. Evaluating how successful services have been at meeting performance targets should be done systematically and the process continuously reviewed and updated.

Another key aspect of performance monitoring is to build up a customer profile of who is using the services on offer, in order to establish how successful the service is in meeting the needs of all sections of the community. Equality monitoring should be carried out, by gender, age, disability and ethnic origin where possible. Performance targets should clearly include the expected level of service uptake by target groups.

The work-force

There is clearly a link between the providers of service and the nature of services provided. An organization's workforce that is representative of the local community will be able to reflect and serve the needs of the community in a much more sensitive manner. This applies not only to the total number of people employed but also to the capacity in which they are employed. It is important to ensure that all levels of the workforce are representative of the community served as a whole in terms of ethnicity, gender and disability.

Codes of practice on family policies in recruitment and selection should be established which set appropriate targets and give guidance on ways of achieving them. Customer care initiatives need to be developed which enhance the attractiveness and accessibility of the organization as an employer and which encourages people to apply for jobs.

An organization's greatest resource is its staff. Organizations striving for quality therefore need to invest in and develop that resource to maximize its potential and increase the satisfaction of staff themselves. Training and employee involvement are important components of the quality initiative.

Customer care training programmes are necessary, particularly for front-line staff in order to understand an organization's customer service objectives, to become familiar with the service standards and complaints procedures, and to learn the skills of dealing with people courteously and effectively face to face, on the phone and by letter.

Employee involvement, at all levels, in guiding policy formation is another essential feature, since employees are the ones in contact with customers every day and therefore well placed to understand how best to improve service delivery.

The way forward

Equality is clearly integral to the concept of quality within the context of an organization's services to its members and to the local community. Further, in developing the process of ensuring good quality services there is much that can be learnt from the experience and expertise developed through equalities initiatives.

Equalities work has pioneered many of the components of what is now recognized as the essential pillars for ensuring good quality services. It is within the framework of equalities work in recent years that elaborate community legislation mechanisms were developed, pioneering work on monitoring systems carried out, complaints procedures set in place, and many imaginative schemes to open up and make more accessible various aspects of organizational policy were begun.

All these are of vital importance in developing family-friendly programmes and policies, setting performance indicators and establishing quality assurance as part of establishing good quality services. What is needed now is to build on and develop these areas to make the provision of quality services by large and small employers a reality in keeping with promoting democracy, accountability and equity.

Flexible Working Patterns

While most debate is focused on the advantages and disadvantages of various childcare options such as nannies, childminders, au pairs, mother's helps and day nurseries, very little attention is paid to the benefits reaped by employers who introduce flexible working arrangements.

In light of the growth in single income families and the steady rise in the cost of living, it's amazing that we still view encouraging women to stay at home as a realistic option. When we consider skill shortages and demographic influences, it's amazing that employers still consider the introduction of flexible working arrangements and parent-friendly employment policies as an optional rather than essential factor in human resource management. The facts speak clearly for themselves. Seventy two per cent of all women of working age have a paid job and make up 44 per cent of employees. Women with a child under 5 comprise the only group where most are not working, but the moment the school doors open, 70 per cent are off collecting a wage. By the time the youngest child is aged 10 or over, 81 per cent are at work, with a rapidly growing shift to full-time employment. This shift might have occurred earlier if more employers recognized their role in making the workplace environment more conducive to combining the roles of parenthood with those of an employee. In the UK, childcare services available free of charge to parents of children under school age fare badly, in comparison to the rest of the EU. Only 2 per cent of the UK's 0- to 2-year-olds have places in publicly funded nurseries. The difficulties of combining parenthood with full-time paid employment in a country which has paid little more than lip service to this issue, probably accounts for the fact that a higher percentage of women in the UK work part time than in the rest of the EU. In fact, according to the Department of Employment, there are 5.5 million part-time employees in the UK. The overwhelming majority are women earning just a little over 75 per cent of men's hourly earnings.

Certain options are available; some are open to all women, such as full-time self-employment, a mixture of self-employment with part-time employment, co-operatives, working from home, teleworking; others are particularly suited to combining employment with childcare, such as negotiating term-time only contracts, job sharing, career breaks, and flexi-time. Falling birth rates in the 1960s and 1970s have produced a decline in the number of school leavers entering the labour market; according to the Department of Employment, 90 per cent of the new jobs in the 1990s will have to be filled by women if they are to be filled at all. This is largely due to the decline in traditional manufacturing industries, where large numbers of men have been employed, and the growth of the service industries, where women have a well-established foothold. The major 'untapped' source of labour for companies experiencing staff and skill shortages will be women who would like to return to the full-time work after having children, but are currently far too often prevented from doing so by lack of childcare. These demographic changes mean that companies will need to attract women with childcare responsibilities back to work during the 1990s. Increasingly companies are being persuaded to be more imaginative in their response to women's needs, in returning to work after maternity leave or a career break, particularly in the south-east of England where the skills shortages are most acute.

Good employers do not happen by accident. The companies in which women do best are those with well-thought-out equal opportunities policies, and which have a range of options on offer to women and men in order to match their working hours to the requirements of the company concerned. In some companies, such as Legal & General, London Weekend Television, ICL, Esso and American Express, the ability to work flexible hours is becoming much more of the norm rather than the exception. American Express has set itself the goal of being the best place to work. Its policy is to be as flexible as possible to enable parents to balance their work and their home life commitments so that they can give their best to the company. In July 1990 it conducted a 'work and home life' survey. Staff were asked how they thought the company could help parents combine work and domestic responsibilities. Top of the list came a workplace nursery. So American Express joined forces with a local well-established childcare company in Brighton, close to its main office, and opened the Amex-Early Years Nursery. Over 70 per cent of staff have said that the provision of the nursery has significantly affected their loyalty to the company. American Express is also working towards after-school care for older children, and subsidized places on holiday schemes. As well as these initiatives in childcare, the company has also introduced comprehensive flexible working policies for employees. These include flexi-time, home-working and teleworking, job sharing, school term contracts, part-time and shift working, and extended leave.

It is not a one way process: these companies and others like them benefit as well as the women. It is becoming increasingly evident in those companies which have tried and tested various working methods outside of the established nine to five, five-day-week pattern that there is no reason why every job needs to be done in this way. In areas which are suffering acute skills shortages such as highly technical jobs, maths and science teaching, specialist computer programming and biotechnology, it is becoming more feasible to negotiate hours on the employee's terms. Further, the average skills content of work in all sectors will increase in the coming years. This process will favour women, who will make up over 80 per cent of the additional employees seeking work in the period up to 1995.

Where childcare arrangements are applied individually as opposed to collectively, women are likely to suffer guilt. Ideally women need to get together and agitate for change, not to feel that they have to be ten times as good as a man to feel legitimate at work. Also, women negotiating a deal for flexible hours need to ensure that they are covered by the company's union or staff association's agreement and are entitled to all other benefits negotiated by such a body, where one exists.

The advantages to employers of flexible working arrangements can be broken down into five points which we will examine in turn. It is important to remember, however, that most benefits overlap, in the same way as the difficulties encountered by women with children returning to work to an unsympathetic employer also frequently overlap.

Recruitment

Childcare and parent-friendly policies attract staff. In a climate where the emphasis is on achieving a well-trained workforce this fact should not be overlooked. The key to any successful business is in making correct recruitment decisions. If an organization gets the selection right, attracting the people who will do the job properly, they will bring the right performance. Having the right people with the right skills in the right job justifies any expense of an equal opportunities policy. At the heart of any equal opportunities programme lies the recruitment policy; recruitment must be entirely based on selecting a person on his or her ability to do a job, and not on any irrelevant and possible discriminatory detail about his or her domestic arrangements.

Organizations which get it right in the first place – before any expensive and distressing mistake are made – have a much lower turnover rate, and of course, there is better continuity. This helps organizations to plan future products and services without the disruption entailed in constant recruitment drives and changes of staff. Also, of course, it means that any investment in training employees is made all the more worthwhile when they are content to stay within the organization.

Retention

Women are far more likely to return to work to the same company after maternity leave or a career break if childcare is offered, or working arrangements can be negotiated which take into account employees' home responsibilities. Where costly investments have been made in developing staff through the provision of training courses, any employer with his or her eye on business success does not want to lose key staff. For employers, retaining good staff is the best available opportunity of internalizing accumulated training and work experience at a time when the labour market is expected to become tighter. In an increasingly competitive European market in which key staff are being lured by the prospect of working in other EU countries, retaining important personnel has become more important than ever before.

Company image

In an age when, whether we like it or not, the packaging often counts more than the product itself, company image is an important issue to bear in mind. Flexible working practices and help with childcare are the essential ingredients of a caring company that wishes to project a good company image. Evidence shows that companies providing a supportive working environment and having regard in their employment practices to the needs of the whole person and not just the employee get far more out of their staff in terms of motivation, loyalty, low rates of absenteeism; all factors which contribute to job performance and productivity. A well-motivated workforce and high morale is clearly going to have a direct influence on the ways in which the company operates and individual members participate in company life.Companies which encourage flexibility and allow staff to inject their own ideas about working practices, rather than rely merely on the established organizational norms, are doing themselves an enormous favour: participation in company decision-making may well be the best way to avoid or reduce the negative effects of the notorious NIH (Not Invented Here) syndrome. Experience shows that if an employee offers an idea, even a ridiculous or hackneyed one, the company should be able to detect in it a positive thread – however tenuous. If taken up and handled well it could encourage commitment to company goals. In turn this enhances company image.

Cost effectiveness

To recruit and train an employee is often a very costly matter. To lose that employee after making that investment in her career development is a waste of money, which in today's economic climate, no organization can afford. The Midland Bank estimates that it loses £17,000 in recruitment, training and management costs for every employee who does not return after maternity leave.

In many organizations which work standard nine to five hours workplace nurseries are ideal for staff, since they enable them to combine employment with the knowledge that their child is being cared for in the same building. The benefits to employers include:

- retaining key staff;
- reduction in absenteeism due to childcare difficulties;
- an increase in company loyalty when staff see that their welfare is taken seriously;
- fewer disruptions in the business calendar as employees with children do not have to take time off during all the school holidays.

And for employees with children:

- They benefit from a high standard of nursery care.
- Their children gain all the benefits of professional nursery care.
- The doors are open to mothers who can continue to breastfeed babies without too much disruption.

One problem is what to do with children over 5 during the school holidays. Some workplace nurseries run holiday play-schemes, for instance the BBC, some parts of the Civil Service and Refuge Insurance. These are also cost effective for employers since they ensure that there is better continuity, due to less absence for domestic reasons. Also, in industries such as retail, hotels, catering and the leisure industry where staff are mostly required at the peak holiday periods, after-school and holiday play-schemes ensure there is additional cover.

Equal opportunities

Assistance with childcare and the provision of flexible working arrangements to enable parents to combine employment with parenthood encourages equality of access to all employment opportunities. This is essential if organizations are going to succeed, since the best way of becoming successful is to encourage each and every member of staff to realize his or her maximum potential. This is the most effective way of stimulating maximum job performance.

Women and people with disabilities are often considered unsuitable for certain types of work. In many firms the fact that women have children makes them a liability and often a short-term prospect. All this is, of course, blind prejudice in the face of evidence which shows that women are as efficient and effective as men and that a disabled worker's output often exceeds that of his or her non-disabled peer. However, a company which has not examined its prejudices still acts on them. The danger here is that although the temptation might be to recruit and promote staff in one's own image, the organization risks overlooking or ignoring the best person for the job.

It is essential that all organizations become equal opportunities employers. An equal opportunities policy might simply be a few lines stating that all employees are treated fairly regardless of gender, race, disability, sexuality and age. What is important is that a policy exists and is put into practice; it counts for far more than any amount of expensive glossy publicity material to herald its launch. Fortunately today, more organizations realize that equality of opportunity represents sound economic sense as well as humanitarian sense. In those organizations with a long-standing tradition in the field of equal opportunities provision much of their success is related to their commitment to equality for all employees. A report in 1992 by Sundridge Park Management Centre says that when it comes to job satisfaction, salary and seniority pale in comparison with being treated fairly. The report has produced two overall messages. First, the type of organization affects how careers are managed; second, the way in which careers are managed affects satisfaction and therefore the numbers who leave an organization. So it is clear that organizations who have resisted becoming equal opportunities employers or considered it an expensive luxury or minor side-issue they can afford to ignore, risk losing key staff to companies which have demonstrated better commitment to career development. At the centre of human resource management and career development lies equality of opportunity.

Those organizations which have merely paid lip service to equality and rapidly become complacent once a fine looking policy has been put in place must pay much greater attention from now on. In the future efficient human resource management will be the only way to adapt to economic pressures and assume a leading position. Therefore, not a little modesty and great circumspection will have to be exercised before each organization feels satisfies with the results of its equal opportunities programme.

Work and Family Life: Reconciling the Differences

Reconciling family life with the economic necessity to work affects millions of women throughout the European Union. The difficulty in achieving this forces many to opt for part-time work, which often affects their promotion chances, or to opt out of the employment market for several years or for ever.

The Head of the Social Security and Social Action Division of the European Commission, which is responsible for family policy, is confident that attitudes are beginning to change and solutions will be found which could be applied EU-wide if the political will was there and if companies found it in their interests.

In 1992 in order to discuss possible ways forward the unit organized a conference with the Belgian Ministry of Employment entitled 'Europe 93, business and the family. What strategies to bring them together?'. For the first time at Community level, the different parties affected by employment and the family were brought together. There were representatives from the international organizations, governments, companies, trade unions and professional organizations. Several questions were posed. Can Europe still afford to maintain an airtight division between work and family life? What are companies doing to harmonize these two worlds? What strategies are firms adopting to encourage the mobility of employees and their families? In answer to these questions a number of key issues were raised and a mixture of strategies which firms were already pursuing and ideas on what could be done in the future were presented. Some of the problems discussed and decisions made were as follows.

1 The success of a company often depends on its ability to be flexible. Applied to the family, flexibility in working hours and how the work itself is organized can give employees more time at home when it was needed. For example, working longer hours on some days means that days off in lieu can be taken with the family. It must be remembered that flexible working arrangements and atypical work gives an economy and society, companies and individuals an indispensable flexibility. Preservation and promotion of flexible work patterns is in the interest of companies and employees and cannot be seen as of secondary importance.

2 Career planning for both female and male employees enables both companies and individuals to plan their careers and negotiate in

advance for part-time work, time off to have children and other family-related temporary absences.

3 Part-time work has to be available for men as well as women and the status of part-time employment has to rise. Too often it is a two edged sword in terms of women and work. On the one hand it promotes the work–family combination to a considerable extent, on the other hand it is a obstacle to development to more demanding positions. Also the lack of infrastructure such as childcare services, efficient public transport, pushes many women into less protected part-time or atypical work; the cost of forcing women into precarious or part-time employment because of lack of back-up services is great. These women's skills are often lost and millions has to be reinvested in retraining and integration programmes. Private initiatives often resolve many of the infrastructure problems: family or neighbours looking after the children, voluntary groups providing school transport and after-school care. There is a need for a mixture of public and private solutions since one of the effects of insufficient infrastructures is that women would opt to have fewer children, with the long-term result of an ageing Europe and a reduced workforce.

4 A number of delegates suggested that there ought to be an unconditional citizen's allowance for those who needed to leave the job market for long or short periods to fulfil personal or family needs. As well as raising the status of the 'carer' it would also have the added advantage of reducing unemployment and would remove the social stigma which is attached to the idea of being without a job.

5 On the important question of mobility many companies have only just started to realize that they have to consider the family as well as the employee when relocating staff. It is clear that many firms are revising their relocation policies to incorporate family responsibility. As an aid to family relocation many companies are introducing familiarization visits of two or three days so that a couple can find accommodation. Language courses are arranged for the employee and his or her partner, and wherever possible a spouse is helped to find work in the new country; some companies offer a bonus to compensate for the loss of a spouse's career. As well as companies including these measures they have to gear their family policy to supporting a changing internal family order, one that reflects that women too have high-grade jobs and are just as likely to be relocated as men.

6 Companies have to contribute to childcare and after-school centres either by contributing to public funds or by pooling resources with other companies.

7 Those men and women who take advantage of flexible work arrangements should have their employment rights and working conditions protected. Parents should have the chance to work shorter hours for a certain period and in-service training should take place during the day or childcare should be provided while it takes place.

Organizers' Schedule for Actions in Companies: Childcare and Family Policies

Employment policies that reflect joint work and family concerns have to be an accurate reflection of what the members of an organization want. If they are written against a background of ignorance they will not respond to the real needs of staff. Consultation and employee participation, examples of which are given below, are essential ingredients of successful policy formulation.

- Arrange for a small team to consult with external organizations who might be useful in advising or assisting in the development and implementation of family and work policies. At the same time make a study of existing equality plans in the company or actions of this type which have already been carried out in the company.
- Consult the relevant trade unions or staff association: the group of affiliated trade unions, the federation of the branch of the industry, union women's groups.
- Prepare arguments and several concise action plans for the implementation of new or revised policy. At the same time, draw up a list of potential fund helpers and supporters.
- Set up a working party to establish a plan of action.
- Prepare a questionnaire on attitudes and opinions on family and work policies.
- Together with the working party, choose a sample group for questioning.
- Send out the questionnaire together with a covering letter guaranteeing confidentiality. Draw up a system of analysis (with outside consultants if necessary).
- Together with the working party, choose a sample group for interviewing.
- Collate and interpret the data with the working party.
- Choices of final aims and plan of action are to be decided with the working party.

- During this time, find visiting speakers who are able to come to the company and talk about equality, sex stereotyping, family policies and flexible working patterns.
- If possible, organize a public debate on this theme with the trade unions and campaign inside the unions (posters, leaflets, articles in the union press).
- Organize seminar groups for staff to prepare for future changes in the company and to draw up individual career plans.
- Plan necessary reorientation and training courses.
- The working party should make an end-of-action evaluation.
- There should be a dissemination campaign amongst employers, company directors, heads of personnel departments, etc.

PART II

Parental Rights and Childcare Provision in EU Member States

Introduction to Part II

This section looks at provision within the European Union for working parents in the event of childbirth, that is, maternity leave, paternity leave, parental leave and leave for family reasons. It also considers the various initiatives in member states for child benefits, family benefits, health matters and childcare provision.

Throughout the European Community statutory maternity leave is a universal right for all employed women. In all but one member state the full period of leave is covered by earnings-related benefits of 70–100 per cent of earnings. The UK is the exception: to qualify for statutory maternity leave a woman must be employed by the same employer for at least two years by the end of the twelfth week before the expected date of birth (if she works for 16 hours a week or more), or for five years if she works for 8–16 hours per week.

Six of the member states have statutory and other provision for paternity leave. These are Belgium, Denmark, France, Luxembourg, Portugal and the Netherlands. Parental leave is statutorily available in nine of the twelve member states. The three without statutory provision are Belgium, Ireland and the UK.

The pregnancy directive is the sixth directive adopted by the Council of Ministers to address equality issues. In the legal area, Article 119 of the Treaty of Rome as well as five directives guarantee the principle of equality in the areas of equal pay, equal treatment in employment and equal treatment in social security matters. Together, they have helped to promote statutory rights and obligations in the member states. They have thus helped to reinforce individual rights and promote significant changes in procedures and terms relating to employment. As a result the Union has an advanced legal framework relating to equal opportunities.

The five directives are:

1 The Equal Pay Directive: the obligation to apply the principle of 'equal pay for work of equal value';
2 The Equal Treatment Directive: prohibiting all sex-based discrimination in employment. By implication it guarantees equal treatment with regard to recruitment, vocational training and promotion;
3 The Social Security Directive: providing for equal treatment in social security schemes. If effectively applied and monitored this is encouraging news for older workers and people approaching retirement age;
4 The Occupational Social Security Schemes Directive: providing for equal treatment in occupational social security schemes;
5 The Self-employment Directive: providing for equal treatment in self-employment.

Besides the five directives the Union has set up a series of eight networks of equality with responsibilities in each member state. They are called EU equality networks, and their creation forms a part of a series of practical measures designed to promote equality. The four main aims of the networks are:

1 The exchange of contacts;
2 the exchange of information;
3 the development of awareness initiatives;
4 the provision of financial support for positive action.

The EU Equal Opportunities Unit in Brussels carries out its policies with the assistance of the eight equality networks. The Equal Opportunities Unit is part of Directorate B (Employment and Labour Market) of Directorate-General V (Employment, Industrial Relations and Social Affairs). The unit is responsible for monitoring the implementation of most equality directives and initiatives and liaises with a number of international bodies about equality matters.

In the framework of the EU Third Action Programme on equal Opportunities Between Women and Men, the Commission will endeavour to bring forward work within the Council regarding the proposals for directives on:

- the burden of proof;
- parental leave;
- statutory and occupational social security schemes.

6

Belgium

Statutory Provision for Maternity Leave

- Paid maternity leave is guaranteed under Articles 39–45 of the law of 16 March 1971 and under Articles 55–76 of the law of 3 July 1978.
- There is no continuous employment requirement.
- Claimants must have a six months' social insurance coverage, including three months preceding confinement, and 120 days of actual or credited work (that is, employment that counts towards receiving any state benefit or assistance).

Entitlements

- Up to six weeks before the birth are granted on request, eight weeks after the birth compulsorily.
- The six weeks allowed before the birth may be taken after the birth instead.
- Employers pay 100 per cent of salary for a certain period depending on employee's status: seven days for blue-collar workers, one month for white-collar workers. Sickness insurance scheme then makes pay up to 100 per cent under collective agreement. Average payments work out at four weeks on 82 per cent and 10 weeks on 75 per cent of salary. The insurance sector, amongst others, allows women an extra one year's unpaid leave.

Statutory Provision for Paternity Leave

- In most sectors new fathers can expect to receive at least two or three days of paid paternity leave. In the public sector many employees are entitled to four days.

- Under Royal Decree, 28 August 1963, the birth or adoption of a child is considered to justify leave of absence.
- Under Articles 88–95 of the law of social recovery of 9 January 1985, employees may request sabbatical leave lasting between six and twelve months provided that:

  (a) it is covered by collective agreement;
  (b) that the employee has at least six months service; and,
  (c) that he or she is replaced by an unemployed person.

  Sabbatical leave covers paternity leave, amongst others.

Entitlements

- Under justified leave of absence, a father is entitled to two days' absence, paid by the employer. If the child is adopted, the parents are entitled to leave equal to the time necessary to fulfil all administrative formalities;
- Full-time sabbatical leave is considered as time worked for the purposes of social security contributions (Royal Decree, 21 March 1985).

Statutory Rights to Parental Leave

No statutory parental leave provisions as such, but under Articles 88–95 of the Law of Social Recovery of 9 January 1985 employees may request sabbatical leave (provided that it is covered by a collective agreement) for amongst other reasons, parental leave.

Entitlements

Sabbatical leave may last between six and twelve months provided that the employee has at least six months' service and that he or she is replaced by an unemployed person. Parents taking time off for the care of a child receive a monthly allowance of 10,504 fr. (approximately £164), or 12,504 fr. (approximately £194) for a second or further child. Under the terms of a Royal Decree of 21 March 1985 it is considered as time worked for the purposes of social security. These provisions cover both the private and public sectors. Sabbatical leave may be taken part time and is not dependent on the age of the child. The employee has the right to return to the same job or to a job at an equivalent grade.

Some collective agreements in the private sector allow men and women to take unpaid leave for up to two years, though in these cases there is no guaranteed right to return to the same job. Employers and employees have always had the right, on an individual basis, to suspend the employment contract by mutual agreement.

Statutory Rights to Leave for Family Reasons

The Royal Decree of 28 August 1963 grants statutory rights for leave for family reasons. Extra unpaid leave is provided for under a national collective agreement of 10 February 1975. Other family leave entitlements have been agreed by collective agreements and cover most occupations.

Entitlements

- death of a close relative: one to three days
- own wedding: two days
- wedding of son or daughter: one day
- ordination, Holy Communion: one day

Paid or unpaid leave is allowed on each relevant occasion.

Entitlements may be increased under collective agreement: the national agreement of 10 February 1975 provided for unpaid leave for family reasons with the details to be negotiated at a sector or company level. For example, the metalworking industry has negotiated for a maximum of five days a year off unpaid.

Childbirth Grants

Childbirth grants can be applied for from the sixth month of pregnancy onwards; it is paid for two months before the expected date of birth as shown on a doctor's medical certificate. In order to qualify for a childbirth grant, it is necessary for a copy of the medical certificate to be enclosed with an application.

Maternity Grants

Payment for maternity grants are derived from employers' contributions and are paid on an income-related scale. Low earners are awarded a full grant for a first child and approximately a 60 per cent grant for any subsequent children. Like childbirth grants, it is essential to apply for these payments, since neither payment is provided automatically.

Family Benefits

Employers and employees are entitled to family benefits for all children up to the age of 14 or until the end of the school year during which they reach that age. Entitlements to family benefits are extended for older children under the following conditions:

- up to the age of 16 for children who are not working;
- up to the age of 21 for young people following a recognized and supervised apprenticeship;
- under certain conditions, up to the age of 25 for a son or daughter who does housekeeping or who helps to keep house if there are at least four children in the household;
- under certain conditions, up to the age of 25, for children or young people attending a secondary school or an establishment of higher education.

There is no age limit for children with a disability or those who are incapable of working.

How to obtain family benefits

In order to receive family benefits, a claim should be submitted to the compensation fund (*Caisse de compensation/Compensatiekas*) of which all employers are a member. Family benefits are paid to the mother by postal money order every month.

Publicly Funded Childcare Provision

Of children under 3, 20 per cent are in publicly funded childcare facilities; of those aged 3 to school age, the proportion is 95 per cent.

Services include nurseries, full-time play groups, services attached to primary schools, kindergartens and crèches.

Health Matters

Anyone who is not paying Belgian national insurance contributions while working in Belgium should take out private medical insurance or could face the possibility of paying the full price of any treatment. Sickness and invalidity benefits are covered by separate funds (*mutualité/mutualiteit*). There is a *mutualité/mutualiteit* office in all major towns. Contributions to these funds are deducted from salaries and paid direct to the insurance company. The costs of medical treatment are in part reimbursed by these sickness insurance funds. About three-quarters of the costs of any fees paid for health services are recoverable.

Sickness benefit

Employees who are unable to work because of sickness must get a doctor's certificate within two days of being unable to work. This certificate should then be sent to the insurance fund to claim sickness benefit. Average benefit rates are 60 per cent of salary for sickness, 79.5 per cent for maternity and approximately 60 per cent for invalidity. Many employers make payments in addition to these benefits so that employees actually receives an amount equivalent to their normal pay.

If an employee has an accident at work, he or she should report it within ten days to the local *mutualité/mutualiteit* office. Claims can be made for incapacity to work, medical treatment and travelling expenses.

Information Points

Accidents at work:	Fonds des Accidents du Travail rue du Trône 100 1050 Brussels
For information on benefits whilst in Belgium:	Office National de la Securité Sociale Boulevard de Waterloo 76 1000 Brussels
Advice on individual rights can be obtained from the Ministry of Employment and Labour:	Inspection des Lois Sociales/ Réglements du Travail Ministére de l'Emploi et du Travail rue Belliard 51–53 1040 Brussels

Belgium Embassy
103 Eaton Square
London
SW1W 9AB

British Embassy
rue d'Arlon 85 Aarlenstraat
1040 Brussels

British Council
10 Spring Gardens
London
SW1A 2BN

British Council
Britannia House
rue Joseph 11 26
1040 Brussels

British Chamber of Commerce for Belgium and Luxembourg
Britannia House
rue Joseph 11 30
1040 Brussels

British Consulate
lange Klarestraat 24
2000 Antwerp

The Belgian equivalent of British jobcentres are:

In Flanders:	Vlaamse Dienst voor Arbeidsbemiddeling (VDAB)
In Wallonia:	Office de la Formation Professionelle de l'Emploi (FOREM)
In Brussels:	Office Régional Bruxellois et de l'Emploi (BGDA/ORBEM)
Head offices:	VDAB Head Office Keizerslaan 11 1000 Brussels
	FOREM Head Office Boulevard de l'Empereur 5 1000 Brussels
	ORBEM/BGDA Head Office Boulevard de l'Empereur 5 1000 Brussels

7

Denmark

Statutory Provision for Maternity Leave

- Paid maternity leave is guaranteed under the law of maternity leave (*Lov om barseloroiv*) of June 1980, amended 7 December 1983.
- There is no continuous employment requirement.
- Claimant must be insured and working for six months during one year preceding confinement, including at least 40 hours in the four weeks preceding leave.

Entitlements

- Four weeks before the birth; 24 weeks after birth.
- The last 10 of these weeks may be taken by either the father or mother or be shared between them.
- Blue-collar workers receive 90 per cent of earnings, up to a maximum of 2,339 kroner (approx £197) a week, for 28 weeks (the first three weeks paid by the employer, then by social security). White-collar employees receive at least 50 per cent for 21 weeks (paid by the employer) within the period between three months before and three months after the birth. White-collar staff receive the equivalent of blue-collar pay as a minimum; public sector collective agreements generally make this up to full pay.

Statutory Provision for Paternity Leave

- Paid paternity leave is guaranteed under the law of maternity leave.
- There are no length of service or other requirements for eligibility.

Entitlements

- Two weeks after the birth or arrival of the child at home.
- This entitlement may be extended by up to 10 weeks (see above under maternity entitlements).

Statutory Rights to Parental Leave

Parental leave provisions were introduced in July 1984 and became fully operative from July 1985 (under law no. 234 on maternity leave of 4 June 1980, amended by law no. 573 of 7 December 1983).

Entitlements

Ten weeks' leave for either parent (but not both simultaneously) can be taken after the existing 14 weeks of maternity leave. Pay is made up to 100 per cent of normal earnings up to a maximum of 2,339 kroner (approx £197) per week. These provisions cover all workers in both private and public sectors, and there are no length of service requirements. Adoptive parents are also covered.

Statutory Rights to Leave for Family Reasons

There are no statutory rights, though a number of collective agreements do provide for leave for family reasons.

Entitlements

Some agreements allow time off for the death of a near relative. Most agreements (though not, for example, construction) allow one day off with sickness benefit for either the father or mother when their child is ill. There is normally a one-year length of service requirement before any such leave is granted. The age of the child at which entitlement ends varies according to agreement. There is not normally a right to unpaid leave.

Childbirth Grants

A woman who satisfies certain conditions relating to her employment and the level of her income (insurance periods completed in other member states are counted as periods of employment) is entitled to cash benefits for pregnancy and childbirth. Payment of such benefit may at the earliest commence four weeks before the expected date of confinement; it continues for 14 weeks after the birth of the child. Persons seeking to adopt a child may likewise receive cash benefit for 14 weeks after the actual date of adoption.

From 1 July 1984 cash benefit may be paid to the child's parents after the birth or adoption of the child for a total of 20 weeks; benefit for up to six of these weeks may be paid direct to the father. From the same date the father also has a separate entitlement to cash benefit for up to two weeks after the birth or adoption of a child. From 1 July 1985 the period of benefit payment is 24 weeks, and benefit for up to 10 of them may be made payable to the father. Cash benefits for maternity, childbirth or adoption are paid for by the social and health department of the commune. Claims for cash benefits for childbirth or adoption should be submitted to the social and health department within six months of the date of birth or actual adoption. Benefits are paid for one week at a time and amount to 90 per cent of the employee's income.

Family Benefits

Employers and employees are entitled to family allowances. General family allowances (*almindeligt bornetilskud*) are granted for children under 16 years of age. Increased family allowances are paid in lieu of the general allowance for children who are supported by only one person and children both of whose parents receive an ordinary retirement pension or an early retirement pension. The age limit is also 16.

Supplementary family allowances are paid to single persons whose children receive increased family allowances. Regardless of the number of children only one supplementary family allowance is paid to each one-parent family. In general, increased and supplementary family allowances are earnings-related in that their exact amount varies with the parents' taxable income.

A young person's allowance may be paid to 16- and 17-year-olds. The amount payable and the period for which the allowance is paid are fixed after an assessment of each case and depend on the expected income of the family during the period in which the allowance is paid and also on the young person's own income.

How to obtain family benefits

Family allowances are paid in respect of the child. They are paid in advance every quarter to the child's mother. Normally, general family allowances are paid automatically without the need to claim. Supplementary and increased family allowances in respect of children who are supported by only one person can only be granted after a claim has been received. Claims must be made to the commune. A young person's allowance can be granted only on submission of a claim to the social and health department of each commune. Details of the family's income and the number of children in the household as well as any other relevant information should be entered on the claim form. The rate of allowances and the period for which they are paid are determined by the commune.

Publicly Funded Childcare Provision

Of children under 3 years of age, 48 per cent are catered for in publicly funded childcare services; from 3 years to school age, the proportion is 85 per cent.

Services include pre-school clubs attached to primary schools, kindergartens, crèches, nurseries. Many employers provide full-time or part-time workplace nurseries.

Health Matters

The Danish national health service is run by *Det Danske Sygehusvæsen*. Anyone who stays in Denmark on more than a tourist basis must have a personal code certificate number (*personnummer*) which is issued by the civil register authorities (*Folkeregisteret*). At the same time applicants are issued with a social security certificate, or health card (*sygesikringsbevis*), which gives access to the public hospital service. Although visits to hospitals are free, charges are made for visits to a doctor and prescriptions but refunds can be obtained. Anyone who is not contributing to the Danish national insurance fund while working is advised to take out private medical insurance or he or she may have to pay the full price for any medical treatment received. Accident insurance is fully financed by employers but administered by the *Socialministeriet*, who make decisions on entitlements. Any employed person is covered. Anyone who suffers an accident at work or work-related illness should notify his or her employer in the first instance.

Sickness benefit

If an employee is unable to work because of sickness he or she must notify the employer as soon as possible and provide a doctor's certificate. Sickness benefits (*sygedagpenge*) are administered by the local social health department (*Kommunens social og Sundhedsforvaltning*) or the Ministry of Social Security.

Information Points

The name and address of the head office of the Danish employment service:	Arbejdsmarkedsstyrelsen Blegdamsvej 56 Box 2722 DK-2100 Copenhagen
Danish Chamber of Commerce:	Det Danske Handelskammer Borsen 1217 Copenhagen
Directorate for Aliens:	Direktoratet for Udlændinge Ryesgade 53 2100 Copenhagen
Civil Register Authorities:	Folkeregisteret CPR Kontoret Datavej 20 Postboks 269 3460 Birkerod
Ministry of Social Security:	Socialministeriet slotsholmgade 6 1216 Copenhagen
For information on health rights:	Arbejdsskadestyrelsen Ebelogade 1 DK 2100 Copenhagen

Royal Danish Embassy
55 Sloane Street
London
SW1X 9SR

British Embassy
Kastelsvej 36
2100 Copenhagen

British Council
Gammel Mont 12, 3
1117 Copenhagen

8

France

Statutory Provision for Maternity Leave

- Paid maternity leave is guaranteed under Article L-122-26 of the Labour Code and Articles L-331-1 to L-332-3 of the Social Security Code.
- There is no continuous employment requirement.
- The applicant must have been registered with social security for at least ten months and either to have worked at least 200 hours in the preceding three months or to have contributed a minimum amount during the preceding six months.

Entitlements

- Six weeks are allowed before the birth, 10 weeks after the birth;
- These entitlements may be increased as follows:
  (a) third or subsequent child: eight weeks before, 18 weeks after;
  (b) multiple births: an extra six weeks before, 12 weeks after for the first two sets of births; an extra six weeks before, 22 weeks after (or split 8 and 20) for subsequent sets of births;
  (c) in case of complications a further two weeks may be prescribed.
- The woman receives 84 per cent of earnings (paid by maternity insurance); most collective agreements make this up to full pay.

Statutory Provision for Paternity Leave

- Paid paternity leave is guaranteed under Article L-226-1 of the labour code.
- There are no eligibility requirements.

Entitlements

- Three days within a period of two weeks around the date of birth are allowed.
- This entitlement may be improved through collective agreement.

Statutory Rights to Parental Leave

Parental leave is guaranteed under the laws of 4 January 1984 and of 29 December 1986, enshrined in Articles L.122-28-1 and following of the Labour Code.

Entitlements

Employees with at least one year's service may request parental leave on the occasion of a birth or adoption and up to the child's third birthday. This leave may be full or half time. In firms employing fewer than a 100 workers the employer may, in certain circumstances, refuse. The leave has two phases:

1 The mother or father may take full- or half-time leave for a maximum period of one year.
2 The leave may then be extended at one-year intervals up to the child's third birthday.

The parent may also change the form of the leave (from half to full time or vice versa). The employee has the right to return to his or her job at the end of the leave. Benefits linked to length of service are halved during leave. Parental leave is unpaid, though the family allowances fund pay an allowance each month to parents taking time off to care for children if the birth or adoption brings the total number of children to three or more. The allowance is dependent on a minimum period of previous employment and is payable until the youngest child's third birthday. In the year before the third birthday, the parent may return to work half time.

Statutory Rights to Leave for Family Reasons

Article L.226-1 of the Labour Code guarantees time off for family reasons. These rights are supplemented by a national agreement of 10 December 1977 as well as sector and company level agreements.

Entitlements

- death of spouse or child: two days;
- death of parent, parent in law, sibling or other close relative: one day;
- wedding of son or daughter: one day;
- own wedding: four days.

Leave is allowed on each occasion.

The entitlements may be increased through collective agreement, and are counted as days worked for the purpose of calculating annual holiday.

Maternity Insurance

Maternity insurance covers:

- medical treatment;
- cash benefit (*indemnités journalières*) during incapacity for work caused by maternity;

The pregnant woman (or the insured person whose insurance covers the benefits she receives) should have been insured for at least ten months before the expected date of confinement.

The pregnant woman is entitled to the following services free of charge:

- prenatal and postnatal examinations (five);
- a maternity belt;
- a preparatory course on painless birth (six lessons);
- confinement care (medical supervision for 12 days);
- medical examinations of the child (12 examinations for the child's first 24 months).

Daily allowances are calculated on the basis of a basic wage or salary. In most cases they are based on the employee's gross earnings during the last month before stopping work. As a rule the daily allowance is paid for the following periods:

- for six weeks before the birth (eight weeks from the third child onwards);
- for 10 weeks after the birth (18 weeks from the third child onwards);
- an extension of the postnatal period by two weeks in the case of multiple births.

Prenatal Allowances

These allowances are payable to all pregnant women regardless of whether or not they are working, provided that:

- within the first 15 weeks of pregnancy they inform the family allowances fund that they are pregnant;
- they undergo three medical examinations during pregnancy;
- they submit certificates stating that they have undergone the examinations to the family allowances fund.

The fund then issues a special booklet for expectant mothers (*carnet de maternité*) which contains all the information on the steps to be taken during this period.

The allowances are paid in three stages: twice the monthly amount in the third month, four times the monthly amount in the sixth month and three times the monthly amount in the eighth month.

Postnatal Allowances

These allowances were formerly known as *allocations de maternité*, i.e. maternity grants. They are awarded on condition that the mother resides in France and undergoes the preventive medical examination at the prescribed times. They are paid in three instalments: at 8 days, 9 or 10 months, and 24 or 25 months after the birth.

Family Benefits

Family benefits provided by French legislation are:

- family allowances (child benefits);
- prenatal allowances;
- postnatal allowances;
- leave for maternity or adoption purposes;
- family supplement;
- family income supplement;
- housing allowance;
- removal grant;
- beginning of the school year allowance;

- special education allowance;
- orphan's allowance;
- single parent allowance.

Entitlements to French family benefits

These arise

- if the claimant and the family are resident in France;
- if at least one child is fully and permanently dependent on the claimant, and, for the award of certain benefits, if his or her income does not exceed a certain fixed amount.

Child benefits (family allowances proper) are awarded from the second dependent child onwards, provided he or she receives a normal school education between the ages of 6 and 16, but certain benefits such as family supplement, orphan's allowance, housing allowance, beginning of the school year allowance and special education allowance can also be obtained for an only child. In certain conditions, benefits are awarded after the age of 16: for children seeking employment for the first time, apprentices, students, etc.

How to obtain family benefits Claims should be submitted to the local family allowances fund (*Caisse d'Allocations Familiales*). For the documents required for each of the benefits listed above, see the guide for beneficiaries (*Guide de l'allocataire*) published by the family allowances fund.

Publicly Funded Childcare Provision

When under 3 years old, 20 per cent of children are catered for in publicly funded childcare services; from 3 years to school age, it is 95 per cent.

Services include pre-school groups attached to infant schools, nurseries and kindergartens.

Health Matters

French social security cover for medical treatment is only partial and it may therefore be wise to take out insurance to cover for the excess charges that may be incurred for medical treatment. In France many insurance companies (*mutuelles*) provide such policies.

French social security covers illness, pregnancy, invalidity, death, accidents at work, job related illnesses and retirement. As soon as a person starts work in France he or she is issued with a social security registration number because the employer will have registered the new employee with the *Caisse d'Assurance Maladie*. In order to receive a social security registration card, apply to the same *Caisse d'Assurance Maladie*.

In general, should medical attention be required in France applications for partial reimbursement of expenses should be made to the nearest *Caisse de Sécurité Sociale* whose address can be obtained from the local town hall (*mairie*). Individuals should ensure that any doctor or dentist who is consulted works within the French sickness insurance scheme (*Conventionné*), otherwise he or she may be liable for the full cost of treatment. The local *Caisse de Sécurité Sociale* keep a list of doctors who charge the official social security rate. After treatment has been completed, the doctor should provide a statement of treatment (*feuille de soins*), which is necessary to claim a refund.

Individuals who are given a prescription should keep the detachable stamps (*vignettes*) on the medicine containers, which show the name and the cost of the medicine. Stick the *vignettes* in the appropriate section of the *feuille de soins* and send this along with the prescription to the *Caisse de Sécurité Sociale* to apply for a refund. In general, refunds of 75 per cent of the cost of medical treatment and 40–70 per cent of the cost of most prescribed medicines are available.

Sickness benefit

Individuals who are unable to work because of sickness must inform their employer as well as the local sickness insurance office, *Caisses Primaires d'Assurance-Maladie*. These offices have overall charge of administering sickness funds.

Information Points

The French equivalent of a jobcentre is the *Agence Nationale pour l'Emploi* (ANPE); the head office is:

ANPE
'Le Galilée'
4 rue Galilée
93198 Noisy-le-Grand

sickness insurance offices:

Caisse Primaire d'Assurance-Maladie de Paris
Service de Relations Internationales
173–175 rue de Bercy
75586 Paris

French Fiscal Attaché
5th Floor
Kingsgate House
115 High Holborn
London WC1V 6JJ

French Embassy
58 Knightsbridge
London SW1X 8SB

British Embassy
35 rue du Faubourg St Honoré
75008 Paris

British Council
9 rue Constantine
75007 Paris

Consulate-General in Edinburgh
11 Randolph Crescent
Edinburgh EH3 7TT

French Consulate in London
PO Box 520
21 Cromwell Road
London SW7 2ON

9

Germany

Maternity Leave

- Paid maternity leave is guaranteed under the Maternity Protection Law 1968 (*Mutterschultzgesetz*), amended in 1979.
- There are no continuous employment requirements.
- Claimants must have worked for at least nine months (seven months in the case of premature births) out of the previous 12 or have been claiming unemployment benefit.

Entitlements

- Six weeks before the birth, eight weeks after the birth, are allowed.
- Post-natal leave may be extended to 12 weeks in cases of premature or multiple births.
- Maternity allowance is paid by social security up to a maximum of DM 25 (approximately £8.20) a day. When a woman's normal net pay exceeds this figure, the employer must make up the difference between maternity pay and normal pay.

Statutory Provision for Paternity Leave

There is no provision for paternity leave as such. Section 616 of the Civil Code (*Burgerliches Gesetzbuch*) allows special paid leave for personal reasons which is usually taken to include a brief spell of paternity leave. Although there are no entitlements under German law except as noted above, collective agreements, often allow one or two days' paid leave for the father at the time of the baby's birth.

Statutory Rights to Parental Leave

Parental leave is guaranteed under the Childcare Allowance and Leave (*Erziehungsgeld and Erziehungsurlaub*) Law of 6 December 1985.

Entitlements

Employees (including those undergoing vocational training and home-workers) are entitled to parental leave of up to 12 months on the birth or adoption of a child, if the partner of the parent taking leave is employed, registered unemployed or in education. Those taking leave must inform the employer of their intention and of the planned length of the leave at least four weeks before its commencement.

Employees taking parental leave may only be dismissed in exceptional circumstances and with official approval. The state pays an allowance of up to DM 600 (approximately £196) per month to a mother or father responsible for childcare and living with the child, as long as he or she is not working. Civil servants are entitled to three years' leave for family reasons, which may be extended to nine years if they live with and care for at least one child under 18 (or other relative requiring care). The first two years' leave is paid; the first six months at flat rate regardless of income and the remaining 18 months at a reduced rate depending on family income. Alternatively, they can work half time. The combined length of half-time work and leave should not exceed 15 years.

Statutory Rights to Leave for Family Reasons

Leave for family reasons is guaranteed under section 616 of the Civil Code and section 45 of the fifth part of the Social Code (SGB V) of 1989. Collective agreements may improve on these rights.

Entitlements

Section 616 of the Civil Code allows male and female employees leave on full pay for relatively short periods of time. The details are often settled through collective agreement. Under section 45 of SGB V working parents covered by statutory sickness insurance, who take time off to look after an ill child below the age of 8 may claim sick pay when there is nobody else at home. A maximum of five days may be claimed each year. This only applies when the parent is excluded from the right to time off. A unique example of such eligibility is Germany is wedding anniversaries, for which one day's leave is granted each year.

Maternity Allowance

Maternity allowance is paid for six weeks before and eight weeks after confinement; it is paid at a rate corresponding to the average net earnings during the last 13 weeks or the last three months. The minimum rate is DM 3.50 and the maximum rate DM 25 per day. No maternity allowance is paid to women who continue to receive their normal wage or salary.

Child Benefit

Persons entitled to benefit: subject to the conditions laid down by the Federal Law on child benefit (*Kindergeld*) all employed and self-employed persons who have their residence or habitual domicile in Germany are entitled to child benefit for their children.

Rate of benefit

Monthly rates are as follows (1992 figures):
DM 50 for the first child;
DM 70–100 for two children;
DM 140–220 for three children;
DM 140–240 for four or more children.

The rate of child benefit for the second and subsequent children is linked to the parents' income. The maximum rate is reduced according to a staggered scale, starting with married couples with two children and an annual net income of DM 42,000 and married couples with three children and an annual net income of DM 49,800. For each additional child the income limit goes up by DM 7,800 per annum.

Eligibility for benefit

Parents of children up to the age of 16 qualify for child benefit if the children are:

- legitimate, legimated and adopted;
- illegitimate;
- stepchildren, foster children, and grandchildren and brothers and sisters on certain conditions.

Parents of children over the age of 16 qualify for child benefit if the children are:

- unmarried;
- married, divorced or widowed and who are principally supported by the parent on account of the fact that their spouse cannot adequately maintain them or because the spouse is not obliged to maintain them, or because, as a widow or widower, they do not receive adequate survivor's benefits.

The following conditions apply in the case of children over the age of 16:

- upper age limit of 27 for children;
- children still at school or receiving vocational training, with income as a vocational trainee not exceeding DM 750 per month;
- spending a year doing voluntary welfare work;
- working exclusively as the sole help of the person running the home of the child benefit claimant if the household includes four or more children;
- running the home, if the household includes at least one other child, in the place of the person normally running the home during a period in which the latter is unfit for work because of illness lasting more than 90 days;
- upper age limit of 18 in respect of children who are not attending school or vocational training but who within the territory of the Federal Republic are registered with the employment office as applicants for vocational training or who are registered as available for employment, provided that their income does not exceed DM 240 per month.

There is no age limit in respect of children who are unable to support themselves on account of physical, learning or psychological disabilities.

How to claim child benefit

Child benefit is granted after written application only. Employed persons should claim using the special form entitled *Antrag auf Kindergeld fur auslandische Arbeitnehmer*. Non-German-speaking applicants should ask their employer, a colleague knowing both German and their language, or someone else who is in a welfare position, for assistance in completing the claim form. Completed forms should be returned to the employment office (*Arbeitsamt*).

If both parents are entitled to claim child benefit, it will be paid to either of them, as designated by common consent.

Documents required The following documents should be sent in together with a claim form:

- an official certificate from an authority (if necessary in the home country) confirming that the children listed on the claim form are still alive (e.g. a civil registry document relating to the members of the family or household);
- for children living in other EU member states, Community Form E401 should be used instead, available from employment offices.

Payment Child benefit is paid regularly at two-monthly intervals, in the course of the second month of the period to which the benefit relates. The payments are made into an individual's account or into his or her employer's account. For each payment received, written notification showing the amount transmitted and the period for which it is paid is provided.

Publicly Funded Childcare Provision

Of children under 3 years old, 3 per cent are catered for in publicly funded childcare services; from 3 years to school age, the proportion is 70 per cent.

Services include pre-school groups attached to infant schools, nurseries, crèches, and in the larger cities and towns kindergartens are common.

Health Matters

Employers are responsible for registering their employees with the sickness insurance fund (*Krankenkasse*) which in turn informs the competent pension and unemployment insurance bodies. After the registration period has been completed the insurance company sends its members an insurance identity card (*Ausweis*) which is required for all future communication with insurance fund holders.

The accident insurance scheme protects individuals while at work or while travelling to and from work. This protection includes measures to prevent accidents and to provide insurance cover in case of injury.

Entitlement to benefits arise on the occurrence of an accident at work; occupational diseases give rise to the same entitlement as accidents at work. Employers are obliged to report all accidents to the relevant professional or trade association.

Sickness benefits

The sickness insurance (general scheme) protects individual members as well as their families in the case of illness. It comprises the following benefits: care of the sick, i.e. medical and dental treatment, supply of medicines, bandages and dressings, aids and appliances, spectacles, nursing at home, cash sickness benefit and domestic help. When an individual becomes unfit for work as a result of illness, his or her employer will usually continue to pay the wage or salary during the first six weeks of incapacity for work. Incapacitated workers who do not enjoy the continued payment of their wage or salary by their employer are eligible for cash benefits (*Krankengeld*), payable by the sickness fund. The rate of this benefit is 80 per cent of the last regular wage or salary.

Information Points

The international section of the German employment service head office:

Zentralstelle Für
Arbeitsvermittlung (ZAV)
Fueurbachstrasse 42-46
6000 Frankfurt am Main 1

German Embassy
23 Belgrave Square
London SW1X 8PZ

German Consulate General
Westminster House
11 Portland Street
Manchester M60 1BY

British Council
Hahnenstrasse 6
5000 Cologne

Chamber of Commerce/Industrie-und Handelskammer
British Chamber of Commerce
Heumarkt 14
5000 Cologne

German Consulate General
16 Eglington Crescent
Edinburgh EH12 5DG

Anglo-German Association
17 Bloomsbury Square
London WC1A 2LP

10

Greece

Statutory Provision for Maternity Leave

- Paid maternity leave is guaranteed under law 1302 of 29 October 1992, which ratified the International Labour Office Convention no. 103 on maternity protection (1952).
- There are no continuous employment requirements.
- Contributions for 200 days are needed during two years preceding entitlements to benefit.

Entitlements

- Six weeks before the birth; six weeks after the birth. This period was extended to a total of 15 weeks under the 1989 central agreement.
- These entitlements may be increased under collective or individual agreement.
- Public servants have the right to four months' paid maternity leave (two months before the birth and two months after the birth).
- A woman receives 100 per cent of normal earnings during maternity leave, paid by social security.

Statutory Provision for Paternity Leave

There is no statutory provision for paternity leave, and no major collective agreements at sector or company level covering this issue.

Statutory Rights to Parental Leave

Paternal leave is guaranteed under law 1483/84 dated 8 October 1984 on the protection of workers with family responsibilities. It covered only the private sector and was extended to the public sector by Presidential Decree 193/88.

Entitlements

A working mother and a working father in a two-parent family are entitled to three months of unpaid leave each, and a single parent is entitled to six months of unpaid leave, until the child is 2½ years old. The parent must have at least one year's service and work in a firm employing at least 100 workers. This leave, which is permitted for each birth provided that at least one year has elapsed since the previous time off, may also be taken by adoptive parents. It is to be taken after maternity leave. The percentage of workers absent on parental leave may not exceed 8 per cent of the total workforce and is allocated on a 'first come, first served' basis. Workers must pay all social security contributions during their absence – their own plus the employer's – if they wish to maintain contributions. They have the right, however, to return to the same job or an equivalent one, not an inferior job.

Statutory Rights to Leave for Family Reasons

Law 1483/84 which deals with parental leave also deals with leave for family reasons.

Entitlements

Time off is allowed in cases of serious illness of husband, wife, dependent relative or child (aged under 16), or in cases of a child's mental illness. Time off is also allowed to visit a child's school. Maximum entitlement over the year, for whatever purpose, is six days, raised to eight and ten days if there are two or more children in the family respectively. Customs and practices in Greece often predate the law in allowing time off for a range of family reasons, including bereavement, weddings and so on.

Maternity Insurance

Maternity benefits are granted on the birth of a child. They consist of:

- a birth grant;
- pregnancy and confinement grants (maternity allowance), exclusively for directly insured women.

Entitlements to birth grant

The birth grant may be claimed by:

- women who are directly insured or who are receiving a pension;
- men who are directly insured or are receiving a pension and whose wife is also covered by their insurance as one of their dependants.

Birth Grant

A flat-rate sum is paid on the birth of a child (confinement) by the national health system (IKA). In order to receive this birth grant, the insured person's health book or the family health book of the wife of an IKA-insured person or an IKA pensioner should be submitted, together with the official birth certificate of the new-born baby. The qualifying conditions are the same as for the granting of sickness benefits in kind.

Maternity Allowance

If a woman is directly insured she is entitled to maternity allowance (i.e. pregnancy and confinement grant). The amount of the pregnancy and confinement grant is the same as that of cash sickness benefit, plus the appropriate increases in respect of dependants. There is no upper limit for the maternity allowance. The allowance is paid, as long as she is not working:

- for 42 days preceding the expected date of delivery (pregnancy grant);
- for 42 days following the birth of the child (confinement grant).

Qualifying conditions for maternity allowance

In order to obtain the pregnancy and confinement grant a woman should have completed at least 200 days of work during the past two years before confinement. The second qualifying condition is that a woman is effectively interrupting her employment.

Family Benefit

Employed persons who are insured with the IKA, the OAED, or another statutory insurance scheme, are entitled to family benefit payable by the Labour Employment Office (OAED), in respect of children residing in Greece or in another member state.

Qualifying conditions for benefit

Individuals are entitled to family benefit if the following conditions can be met:

- he or she is an employed person with at least one dependent child;
- he or she has completed 50 days of employment within the preceding calendar year, and has paid the corresponding contributions.

The collective wage agreement by which an individual is covered does not oblige the employer to pay family benefits (5 per cent of the wage, provided that this amount is at least equivalent to the OAED benefit rate).

Persons entitled to family benefit

The parents (father or mother) in respect of their unmarried dependent children, provided that the latter are:

- under 18 years of age;
- under 22 years of age and still studying;
- unfit for work (regardless of age).

The grandfather or grandmother, brother or sister, uncle or aunt, are entitled to benefit in so far as he or she is supporting full orphans or children with only one surviving parent and, in the case of the latter, the surviving parent does not qualify for family allowance.

Children entitling their parents to family benefit are Legitimate children, legitimated children, recognized children, adopted children and also illegitimate children if their mother is already entitled to benefit. The mother is considered entitle to benefit if she fulfils the necessary conditions and if the father for some reason or other is not entitled to OAED benefits.

Benefit

A family allowance is paid from the birth of a first child in respect of all children who qualify for benefit, the amount of benefit depending upon how many children a family has. The family allowance is higher for the second child than for the first, and higher for the third than for the second, but from the third child onwards the allowance remains the same. The allowance is calculated for each insured day of work; the monthly amount is obtained by multiplying the daily benefit by 26.

Family benefit is increased by 100 per cent for each of the first two children, and by 50 per cent for each additional child, if the person entitled to benefit is widowed, or if the father is carrying out military service and the mother is entitled to benefit, and in so far as the person entitled to benefit is not drawing survivors' pension and the spouse is not drawing invalidity pension.

In order to draw family allowance in respect of children living in a member state other than Greece, an E 401 form must be submitted with each claim, showing a family's composition. Further information on family benefits may be obtained from local OAED offices.

Publicly Funded Childcare Provision

Of children under 3 years old, 4 per cent are catered for in publicly funded childcare services; from 3 years to school age, the proportion is 70 per cent.

Both the range and standard of available services varies significantly throughout Greece; the capital Athens and other major cities such as Thessalonika are well served with the complete range of childcare services including infant schools, pre-school groups attached to infant schools, publicly funded nurseries, crèches, and kindergartens. In rural Greece, however, there is very little publicly funded childcare for pre-school-aged children; as a consequence many children remain with their families full time until they commence primary school.

Health Matters

The Greek national health system is run by *Idrima Kinonikon Asfalisseon* (IKA). The IKA deals with health, sickness, maternity and old age benefits whilst the OAED (Greek Manpower Employment Organization) deals with unemployment and family benefits. Social security contributions are deducted at source by employers and paid to IKA. It is an employer's responsibility to register with the social security fund and issue each employee with a booklet or papers which feature the title DATE (insurance and contribution card).

For individuals who are not paying Greek national insurance contributions, it is advisable to take out private medical insurance or face the possibility of paying the whole cost of any treatment themselves.

When an employee starts work he or she must obtain a medical booklet (*iatrico vivliario*) from a local IKA office which must be taken on all visits to doctors or hospitals. Local IKA offices can provide a list of doctors who work within the national health system.

Doctor and hospital treatment within the Greek national health system is free. Patients pay a quarter of prescription charges. Individuals in remote parts of Greece that are not covered by a local IKA office have to pay the cost of any private medical treatment and make a claim for the cost from the IKA office in Athens after receiving treatment. However, refunds are only a proportion of the cost and patients are responsible for the balance. Receipts and documentation are required in order to make a claim. If an individual has an accident at work he or she should notify the local IKA office within five days.

Sickness benefits

Individuals who are unable to attend work due to sickness should notify their employer. Claims for sickness benefits are made via employers to the local IKA office.

Information Points

The Greek equivalent of a UK jobcentre is an office of the Manpower Employment Organization (*Organisimos Apasholisseos Ergatikou Dynamikou*, OAED).

The European Employment Services (EURES) is based at OAED Head Office:

OAED
Ethnikis Antistasis 8
16610 A. Kalamaki

For information on Greek companies contact:

Emborika & Viomichaniko Epimelitino Athinon (EBEA)
Akadimias 7-9
106 71 Athens

IKA
Tmima Diethon Scheseon
Kifissias Avenue 178
152 31 Athens

Ypourgio Ergassias (Ministry of Labour)
Tmima Diethon Scheseon
Piraeus Street 40
101 82 Athens

Greek Embassy
1a Holland Park
London W11 3TP

British Embassy
1 Ploutarchou Street
106 75 Athens

British Council
Filikis Etairias 17
Kolonaki Square
106 73 Athens

11

Ireland

Statutory Provision for Maternity Leave

- Paid maternity leave is guaranteed under the Maternity Protection of Employees Act 1981 and the Social Welfare (Amendment Act 1981).
- There is no continuous employment requirement.
- The claimant must work 18 hours or more a week and have been in insurable employment for at least 26 weeks.

Entitlements

- A total of 14 weeks is allowed, of which at least four must be before the birth and at least four after.
- These entitlements may be increased by up to four weeks, though these extra weeks are unpaid and subject to compliance with notification requirements.
- The woman receives 70 per cent of gross pay from the Department of Social Welfare.

Statutory Provision for other Kinds of Leave

There is no statutory provision for paternity leave, and there are, so far, no major collective agreements at sector or company level covering this issue. There is also no provision for parental leave.

There is no statutory right to leave for family reasons, although a significant number of arrangements seem to be negotiated locally on the basis of custom and practice.

Maternity Benefits

There are two maternity allowance schemes.

The maternity allowance scheme for women in employment

applies only to women who are on maternity leave from their full-time employment and who are entitled to resume work with the same employer at the end of the maternity leave period.

The allowance under the general scheme is payable to insured women who do not qualify under the scheme for employed women.

Periods of insurance, residence or work which the insured woman has completed in other member states may be aggregated to enable her to satisfy the qualifying conditions for allowances under either scheme.

To claim maternity allowance the woman concerned should obtain a special form from the Department of Social Welfare, have it completed by her doctor and her employer (if she is employed) and return it to the Department of Social Welfare.

The allowance is payable to employed women for a period of 14 weeks. The allowance under the general scheme is paid for 12 weeks; payments are made in the form of a weekly cheque. Under the scheme for women in employment the amount of the allowance is 70 per cent of the woman's earnings in the relevant income tax year, subject to a fixed minimum weekly payment. The relevant income tax year depends on the date of the claim.

The rate of the allowance under the general scheme is equivalent to the maximum rate of disability benefit or unemployment benefit payable to insured persons without dependants and, in addition, the insured woman may receive pay-related benefit.

A woman may also be entitled to all the maternity care services provided by her local Health Board.

Family Benefits

Children's allowances These allowances, which do not depend on insurance or on means, are payable in respect of each child under the age of 16. The age limit is extended to 18 years where the child is receiving full-time education or is incapacitated.

Individuals in insurable employment in Ireland or in receipt of a benefit or pension under Irish law qualify for Irish children's allowances even though the children may be residing in another member state. Any office of the Department of Social Welfare can provide further information.

The allowances are payable monthly and an allowance becomes

payable from the first day of the month following that in which a child is born. Claims should normally be made by the mother of the child within three months of that day on a form available from any post office, otherwise part of the allowance may be lost.

Special lump-sum grants These are made to the mother in the case of multiple births of three or more children. Application may be made in the same way as for an allowance.

Publicly Funded Childcare Provision

Of children under 3 years old, 2 per cent are catered for in publicly funded childcare services; from 3 years to school age, it is 55 per cent.

Services are generally based on pre-school nurseries and small groups for pre-school-aged children attached to existing infant schools.

Health Matters

Ireland's national health service is run by the Department of Health. Medical needs are catered for on a means tested basis, and individuals who satisfy the means tested conditions are entitled to the full range of health services free of charge. Anyone in receipt of a social security pension from another EC member state may also be exempt from medical costs.

If medical assistance is sought during a stay in Ireland claims for medical costs should be made as soon as possible after they have been incurred. In the event of an employee having an accident at work he or she should apply for Injury Benefit within 21 days by obtaining a 'first medical certificate' from any doctor.

Sickness benefit

Sickness benefit must be claimed within seven days of becoming ill by sending a completed 'first medical certificate' and claim form (which is available from all doctors) to the Department of Social Welfare. The Department of Social Welfare administers social security contributions in Ireland. The system is known as Pay-Related

Social Insurance (PRSI). Benefits cover pensions, sickness, unemployment, invalidity and maternity benefits. For employees contributions are deducted from salaries or paid by individuals themselves if they are self-employed. In order to receive sickness benefits the PRS1 contribution conditions have to be satisfied; for individuals who have worked in another EU country previous social insurance contributions are taken into account.

Information Points

British Embassy
33 Merrion Road
Dublin 4

British Council
Newmount House
22–24 Lower Mount Street
Dublin 2

Department of Health
Hawkins House
Dublin 2

Department of Social Welfare
Aras Mhic Dhiarmada
Store Street
Dublin 1

Embassy of the Republic of Ireland
17 Grosvenor Place
London SW1X 7HR

Employment Agencies Section
Department of Enterprise and Employment
Davitt House
65a Adelaide Road
Dublin 2

FAS (The Employment and Training Authority)
27–33 Upper Baggott Street
Dublin 4

Irish Congress of Trade Unions
Head Office
19 Raglan Road
Dublin 4

The Chamber of Commerce of Ireland
22 Merrion Square
Dublin 2

Voluntary Health Insurance Board
VHI House
20/23 Lower Abbey Street
Dublin 1

12

Italy

Statutory Provision for Maternity Leave

- Paid maternity leave is guaranteed under law 1204 of 30 December 1971.
- There is no continuous employment requirement.
- Women must be employed and insured at beginning of pregnancy.

Entitlements

- Eight weeks are allowed before the birth (twelve in case of a physically demanding job or in cases of certified sickness), and 12 weeks after the birth.
- A further six months' leave is optional during a child's first year, as is unpaid parental leave until the child is 3 if it is ill.
- The woman receives 80 per cent of her normal earnings during maternity leave, paid by social insurance, and 30 per cent during optional leave.
- Two hours a day paid time off is allowed until the child's first birthday.

Statutory Provision for Paternity Leave

There is no statutory provision for paid paternity leave, and so far, no major collective agreements at sector or company level covering this issue.

Statutory Rights to Parental Leave

Parental leave is guaranteed under law 1204 of 30 December 1971 (for mothers) and law 903 of 9 December 1977 (for fathers).

Entitlements

The mother or the father may take up to six months' leave during the first year of the child's life. Length of service requirements are unspecified. The parent receives 30 per cent of normal earnings from INPS, the National Institute for Social Security. These rights also apply to adoptive parents, stepparents and guardians acting in place of parents.

There are no central agreements on this issue, but certain sector-level agreements may improve on the legal provisions. Part-time leave is now allowed, and entitlement may be extended until the child is 3 if it is sick (on presentation of a medical certificate). There is also the right to unpaid leave. Parents have the right to return to their job. Parental leave is treated as holiday leave for the purposes of social security.

Statutory Rights to Leave for Family Reasons

Employees in the public sector have a statutory right to leave for family reasons. In the private sector, rights are negotiated through collective agreements.

Entitlements

Most employees are entitled to paid leave of between 10 and 30 days when they get married. Short periods of time off are allowed in cases of, for example, the death of a close relative; three days over the year is normal. Other leave for personal reasons is often regulated through custom and practice.

Maternity Allowance

In order to obtain cash benefits for maternity, pregnant employees should hand in or send (via their employer) to the competent INPS office the relevant application accompanied by a medical certificate confirming pregnancy and a statement from the employer certifying that they have ceased work because of pregnancy.

As soon as the birth has taken place, the child's birth certificate and a certificate relating to the composition of the family (*stato di famiglia*) should be forwarded to the INPS.

Family Benefits

Employees may apply for family allowances, or an increase in them, in respect of the dependent members of their family resident in Italy or in another member state.

Entitlement to these benefits does depend, however, on the amount of a family's total annual income, account being taken of the number of dependent family members.

Family members in respect of whom claimants may receive family allowances are:

- a spouse, provided that his or her monthly earnings do not exceed a certain amount;
- children, provided that they are aged under 18 and are dependent on the claimant;
- the claimant's brothers, sisters and grandchildren, provided that they are aged under 18 and are dependent on the claimant;
- parents and grandparents, provided that they have reached the age of 60 (men) or 55 (women) and provided also that their monthly earnings do not exceed a certain amount and that they are dependant on the claimant.

The above age-limits are raised in the following circumstances.

- If a claimant's children are attending secondary school or are pursuing a vocational training course entitlement to family allowances throughout the period during which they are attending school or pursuing such a course is retained.
- If the children are attending university, the claimant retains entitlement to family allowances for the statutory duration of the course of study but, in any case, not after the children have attained the age of 26.
- If the children, brothers, sisters, grandchildren, parents or grandparents are totally disabled, such that they are unable to pursue a professional or trade activity, family allowance in retained.

A person may claim the family allowance increase for dependent children under 18 years of age in respect of whom family allowances are already being received.

How to obtain family benefits

To claim family benefits employees should submit to their employer a written application on the appropriate form, which is obtainable either from the employer or from a local INPS office. Applications should be accompanied by a certificate on the composition of an individual's family (obtainable from the local authority) which should state the surname, forename and date of birth of each dependent member of a family.

How and when the allowances are paid

Family benefits will normally be paid directly to employees by their employer together with the monthly or weekly wage or salary. This does not apply to farm workers and domestic workers, who receive family benefits directly from the INPS office.

Individuals are entitled to receive family benefits in respect of all periods during which they are working, provided that they are in receipt of a wage or salary. This includes probationary periods, leave, marriage leave, public holidays (excluding Sundays), periods of notice and, under specified conditions, absences from work owing to illness, pregnancy and childbirth, accidents at work, occupational diseases, or for disciplinary reasons.

Publicly Funded Childcare Provision

Of children under 3 years old, 5 per cent are catered for in publicly funded childcare services; from 3 years to school age, it is 85 per cent.

Italy has a whole range of services to cater for the needs of preschool children: nurseries, kindergartens, crèches and play-groups, both full time and part time, are commonplace in major cities and towns as well as in rural districts.

Health Matters

The Italian national health service is run by the *Servizio Sanitario Nazionale* (SSN). Individuals who enter Italy to look for work must, within seven days of arrival, apply for a residence permit (*permesso di soggiorno*) which enables holders to stay in Italy and look for work for up to three months. Once a *permesso di soggiorno* has been obtained, and Italian national insurance contributions are being paid, individuals should register with the local *Unita Sanitaria Locale* (USL) and obtain a national health number. USL addresses can be found in the local newspaper or the *TuttoCittá*, a supplement that comes with telephone directories. Once registered with the USL the next step is to register with a doctor (*medico convenzionato*). A list of doctors, local and national health centres and hospitals is available from local USL offices. Self-employed or freelance workers should register with local offices of the *Istituto Nazionale di Previdenza Sociale* (INPS), which is the main social security office. Social security covers old age, disability, sickness, unemployment benefits and health care. Employers deduct national insurance payments to be paid to INPS from each employee's wage packet.

For individuals who are not contributing to the Italian national insurance fund while working, it is advisable to take out private medical insurance or they could face the possibility of paying the full price of any treatment.

For individuals who pay Italian social security contributions, health benefits include free hospital accommodation. Medical treatment and prescription charges can be very expensive; the amount payable depends on an each person's income. There are additional charges for medical tests and specialist examinations.

All accidents that occur in the workplace must be reported via an employer to the nearest office of the Istituto Nazionale Assicurazione Infortuni sul Lavoro.

Sickness benefits

Sickness benefits are usually paid by employers, who then claim refunds from the INPS. For individuals in receipt of sickness benefits in the UK or another EU country, transfer payments may be made to Italy should they decide to look for work there.

Information Points

National welfare and assistance office for medical practitioners	Ente Nazionale di Previdenza ed Assistenza Medici (ENPAM) Via Torino 38 Rome
National welfare and assistance office for pharmacists	Ente Nazionale di Previdenza ed Assistenza Farmacisti (ENPAF) Viale Pasteur 49 Rome

National welfare and assistance office for veterinarians	Ente Nazionale di Previdenza ed Assistenza Veterinari (ENPAV) Via Antonio Bosio 2 Rome
National welfare and assistance office for midwives	Ente Nazionale di Previdenza ed Assistenza per le Ostetriche (ENPAO) Lungotevere degli Intentori 88 Rome
National welfare fund for engineers and architects	Cassa nazionale di previdenza per gli ingegneri ed architetti Via Rubicone 11 Rome
National welfare and assistance fund for surveyors	Cassa nazionale di previdenza ed assistenza a favore dei geometri Via Cavour 178/A Rome
National welfare and assistance fund for solicitors and barristers	Cassa nazionale di previdenza ed assistenza a favore degli avvocati e dei procuratori Via Ennio Quirino Visconti 8 Rome
National welfare and assistance fund for economists	Cassa nazionale di previdenza ed assitenza a favore di dottori commercialisti Via Purificazione 31 Rome
National welfare and assistance fund for accountants	Cassa nazionale di previdenza ed assistenza a favore di ragionieri e periti commerciali Via Luigi Robecchi Brichetti 11/13 Rome
National welfare and assistance office for employment experts	Ente nazionale di previdenza ed assistenza per i consulenti del lavoro (ENPACL) Viale Oceano Pacifico 44 Rome

There are two Italian equivalents of a UK job centre: an *Ufficio di Collocamento Manodopra* (UCM) or a *Sezione Circoscrizionale per l'Impiego e il Collocamento in Agricoltora* (SCICA). The addresses of local offices can be obtained from a telephone directory or the Italian equivalent of Yellow Pages, *Pagine Gialle*.

British Chamber of Commerce for Italy
Via Agnello 8
20121 Milan

For information on health matters, *Unita Sanitaria Locale* (USL) addresses can be found in local newspapers or the *TuttoCittá*, a supplement that comes with telephone directories.

Self-employed or freelance workers should register with the local *Istituto Nazionale di Previdenza Sociale* (INPS).

Their address in Rome is: INPS
Via Ciro il Grande 21
00144 Rome

Italian Embassy
14 Three Kings Yard
London W1Y 2EH

Italian Consulate-General
38 Eton Place
London SW1 8AN

Italian Consulate-General
111 Piccadilly
Manchester M1 2HY

Italian Consulate-General
32 Melville Street
Edinburgh EH3 7HA

Italian Vice-Consulate
7–9 Greyfriars
Bedford MK40 1HJ

British Embassy
Via XX Settembre 80a
00187 Rome

13

Luxembourg

Statutory Provision for Maternity Leave

- Paid maternity leave is guaranteed in the law of 3 July 1975.
- There is no continuous employment requirement.
- Social insurance covers at least six months during the year immediately preceding confinement.

Entitlements

- Eight weeks are allowed before the birth, eight weeks after it.
- The postnatal entitlement may be increased to 12 weeks in the case of premature or multiple births or for women who are breastfeeding.
- The woman receives 100 per cent of normal earnings during maternity leave.

Statutory Provision for Paternity Leave

There is no paternity leave allowed as such. Under Article 16 of the law of 22 April 1966, which regulates annual paid holidays, the birth of a child is considered to justify leave for personal reasons. Under this, the father is entitled to two days' paid absence. This leave cannot be extended, but there are no eligibility requirements.

Statutory Rights to Parental Leave

Parental leave is guaranteed in the public sector under a law of 14 December 1983 (which modified the law of 16 April 1979). A bill on parental leave in the private sector was given its first reading in June 1983 but has since made no progress.

Entitlements

After maternity leave, women are entitled to terminate their contract of employment without notice. They may apply for re-engagement during the following year and must be given preferential consideration in their application by the employer. The bill referred to above would allow all workers in the private sector to take a maximum of two years unpaid parental leave to look after a child under the age of 3. Such workers would have preferential access to their old job or a similar one without loss of benefits on expiry of their parental leave entitlement. As it is, there are no major collective agreements covering parental leave. In the public sector, employees already have the right to one year's unpaid parental leave or to transfer to part-time work in order to look after a child under the age of 4.

Statutory Rights to Leave for Family Reasons

Leave for family reasons is guaranteed under Article 16 of the law of 22 April 1966.

Entitlements

- death of parent or spouse: three days
- death of an in-law: one day
- wedding of a child: two days
- own wedding: six days
- birth of a child (for father): two days
- moving house: two days

Leave may be taken on each of the above occasions, but only at the time of the event. Entitlements may be improved by collective agreement or custom and practice. Full pay is guaranteed by law.

Childbirth Grants

On the birth of the child, under certain conditions concerning residence and medical supervision, women are entitled to a childbirth allowance (*allocation de naissance*) which is paid partly as a parental allowance, partly as a childbirth grant, and partly as a postnatal allowance.

Family Benefits

Individuals are entitled to family allowances for dependent children:

- as a rule, up to the age of 18;
- up to the age of 25 for children who are still studying;
- without age limit for children with a physical or mental handicap.

The family allowance is withdrawn from the month following the month in which the child got married, unless he or she is still studying.

Type and rates of benefits

Benefits consist of standard family allowances, and supplementary allowances.

The rates of standard family allowances are on a rising scale for each of the first three children. It is fixed for the fourth and any subsequent children. For children from 6 to 16 age supplements are paid. In addition to the standard family allowance, the supplementary allowance is awarded for each child aged under 18 with a physical or mental disability of at least 50 per cent compared with normal children of the same age.

The amount of the supplementary allowance is the same as the standard family allowance payable for the first child. There is no age limit if the child is unable to meet its own needs, provided it is not receiving a pension. Family allowances are adjusted annually in accordance with changes in the cost of living.

Formalities to be completed Individuals should submit a claim to the family allowance fund. Claim forms are available from the fund or from communal administrations. Supporting documents to be enclosed are listed on the claim form.

Payment of allowances Family allowances are paid monthly to the father if the child is being brought up by both parents living under the same roof. If the parents are separated the allowances are paid to whichever parent has actual custody of the child.

Children residing in another member state

Individuals are also entitled to family allowances for any of their children who are being brought up in another member state. This applies to anyone who is employed in Luxembourg or who is temporarily not working but receiving any of the following benefits under the scheme for employed persons:

- cash sickness benefit;
- cash benefits for accidents at work;
- accident pension;
- unemployment benefit.

Publicly Funded Childcare Provision

Of children under 3 years, 2 per cent are catered for in publicly funded childcare services; from 3 years to school age, the proportion is 60 per cent.

Publicly funded services include nurseries, kindergartens and crèches.

Many children are looked after by their parents' employers in workplace nurseries and pre-school play-groups. Many employers also run after-school clubs and holiday groups for children of school age.

Health Matters

The Luxembourg national health service is run by the *Ministère de la Santé*. All hospitals are funded by the Luxembourg government with money from employers and employees' contributions to the sickness insurance funds (*caisse de maladie*). There are nine *caisses de maladie*, each dealing with particular professions.

There are fees for all medical services but 80–90 per cent of these fees can be claimed back from the *caisse de maladie*. Anyone not paying Luxembourg contributions to the *caisse de maladie* while working is advised to take out private medical insurance or face the possibility of paying the full price of any treatment.

All accidents at work must be reported as soon as possible after the event via the employer to the *Assurances-Accidents, Section Industriellees*, based in the centre of Luxembourg.

Sickness benefits

Claims for sickness benefits are made through the *caisse de maladie* which deals with the specific profession. A doctor's certificate stating the nature of the sickness and its likely duration is required. If individuals are in receipt of benefits in another EU country, these benefits may be transferred to Luxembourg.

Information Points

The Luxembourg equivalent of a UK job centre is an office of *l'Administration de l'Emploi*. The head office of the government employment service is:

l'Administration de l'Emploi
38a rue Philippe 11
Boite Postal 23
L-2010 Luxembourg

British Chamber of Commerce for Luxembourg
BP 2740
L-1027 Luxembourg

The Chamber of Commerce for Luxembourg companies is at:	Chambre de Commerce du Grand Duché de Luxembourg 7 rue Alcide de Gasperi L-2981 Luxembourg
For information concerning health rights:	Ministère de la Santé 57 boulevard de la Pétrusse L-2935 Luxembourg
The co-ordinating body for insurance funds (*caisse de maladie*) is:	Union des Caisses de Maladie 26 rue Zithe L-2763 Luxembourg
Accidents at work:	Assurances-Accidents, Section Industrielle 125 route d'Esch L-1471 Luxembourg

Luxembourg Embassy
27 Wilton Crescent
London SW1X 8SD

British Embassy
14 Boulevard Roosevelt
L-2450 Luxembourg

14

The Netherlands

Statutory Provision for Maternity Leave

- Paid maternity leave is guaranteed under the Sickness Law 1967 (*Ziektewet*).
- There is no continuous employment requirement.
- The claimant must have been in paid employment for at least six months to be eligible, though this requirement is often waived by the appropriate Industry Board (*bedrifsvereniging*) which, under Article 44 of the Sickness Law, administers the scheme.

Entitlements

- Six weeks are allowed before the birth, six weeks after the birth.
- There are no provisions for extending this entitlement, though maternity leave may sometimes be extended unofficially with a doctor's note.
- The woman receives 100 per cent of normal earnings during maternity leave; this benefit is administered like sick pay.
- In mid-1988 the government proposed extending leave after the birth to eight weeks. The consultative body, however, was split on the proposal, and its fate is currently uncertain.

Statutory Provision for Paternity Leave

No paternity leave is allowed as such. Under Article 1638c of the Civil Code, the birth or adoption of a child is, however, considered a reason for authorized absence. Under authorized absence, the law provides for one day's paid leave for family obligations and two days' paid leave for the birth of a child.

Statutory Rights to Parental Leave

There are no statutory rights to parental leave. A bill on the subject was tabled in Parliament in mid-1988, but it is still under consideration. Under collective agreements parental leave is available on an unpaid part-time basis for a maximum of six months, to both parents.

The bill referred to above would give all working parents with one year's service the right to unpaid part-time leave to look after children up to the age of 4. They would have to work at least 20 hours per week for their employer. Two parents could take their leave separately or together. The right would also apply to adoptive or long-term foster parents.

Statutory Rights to Leave for Family Reasons

Statutory rights to leave for family reasons are guaranteed under Article 1638c of the Civil Code (*Burgerlijk Wetboek*). Many collective agreements contain provisions for leave in cases of serious family illness. The Civil Code allows one day's paid leave for family obligations, two days for birth of a child or marriage and up to four days for bereavement.

Maternity Benefits in Cash and in Kind

If a pregnant woman is working in the Netherlands and is insured in her own right, she is entitled during pregnancy to maternity benefits (*zwangerschapsuitkering*) equal to her daily wage. The benefit is provided from the sixth week before the expected date of confinement up to the actual confinement.

For six weeks after confinement, she will receive confinement benefits (*bevallingsuitkering*) equal to 100 per cent of her daily wage. After that, sickness benefit can be provided for 46 weeks at the most for individuals who are unable to return to work as a result of the confinement. Applications for these benefits should be made in good time to the professional or trade association to which the employer is affiliated. Pregnant women are further entitled to free obstetric services and partial reimbursement by the sickness fund for maternity care if they are covered by a Netherlands sickness fund insurance scheme (*ziekenfondsverzekering*). An employer's sickness fund can provide additional information. Women who wish to use the services of a maternity care centre (*kraamcentrum*) should contact a medical welfare organization (*kruisvereniging*) not later than five months before the expected date of confinement.

Family Allowances

Individuals who live or work in the Netherlands are normally entitled to family allowances from the first child onwards. They are entitled to family allowances for their own children, stepchildren and foster children aged under 16, if they are dependants as defined by Netherlands legislation.

In certain cases, this age limit can be raised to 18 years for handicapped children and up to 27 years for children pursuing a course of studies or vocational training.

Under certain conditions, one child may count as two or three children for the purposes of entitlement to family allowances. As a rule, one child counts for two if the child in question is pursuing a course of studies or is handicapped and is supported mainly by the claimant. One child counts for three where the child in question is pursuing a course of studies, does not reside in the claimant's home and is supported entirely or almost entirely by the latter.

Date of entitlement Entitlement to family allowances is conditional upon the claimant being insured on the first day of the quarter in which the claim is submitted. The qualifying conditions for family allowances must also be satisfied by that date.

Amount of family allowances The amount of the family allowance depends upon the composition of the family on the first day of the relevant quarter.

Claims for family allowances In order to claim family allowances individuals should submit a completely filled in and signed claim form to the Labour Council (*Raad van Arbeid*) in their place of residence. The necessary forms are obtainable at any post office and from the Labour Councils.

When the mother and father are married either can claim for children living with them. Where the parents are divorced or separated, the claim should be made by the parent who cares for and brings up the children. Claims should be submitted not later than three years after the quarter for which the family allowance is applied for.

Publicly Funded Childcare Provision

Of children under 3 years, 2 per cent are catered for in publicly funded childcare services; from 3 years to school age, it is 55 per cent.

Services include pre-school play-groups and 'small schools' for pre-primary school children, nurseries and kindergartens.

Health Matters

The Dutch health system is administered by the Health Service. Free medical treatment is available to those people whose income does not exceed a fixed amount, which is determined each year. Free treatment includes medical aids and appliances, dental treatment, drugs, medicine, dressings, treatment in hospital and transporting costs.

There is no independent insurance scheme in the Netherlands for accidents at work or occupational diseases. Individuals who are incapable of work as a result of an accident are entitled to sickness benefit for a year. Thereafter a doctor's examination and report should be obtained in order to ascertain eligibility for disablement benefits.

Sickness benefits

In the Netherlands sickness benefits are administered by the Ministry of Social Affairs and Employment. Local social security offices can be located via telephone directories or through the local employment offices or job centres (*Arbeidsbureau* or AB). Alternatively the Social Insurance Information Centre in Amsterdam can supply details of benefit entitlements.

For individuals in receipt of sickness benefits in another EU country payments may be able to be transferred to the Netherlands. In the UK, local Department of Social Security (DSS) offices can provide further information, and elsewhere, European Information Centres (EICs) can supply the necessary details. For non-Dutch applicants the foreign affairs department of the Health Service known as ANOZ (*Afdeling Buitenland can het Zietenfonds*) can provide information on health matters and benefit entitlements pertaining to foreign residents.

Employees unable to work as a result of sickness or an accident are entitled to sickness benefit payable by the professional or trade association to which their employer is affiliated. In order to be eligible individuals should report sick as soon as possible to their employer who will then inform the professional or trade association. Sickness benefit amounts to at least 80 per cent of an individual's wage or salary, subject to a ceiling. It is provided for a maximum period of 52 weeks from the third day of illness.

Information Points

The Dutch equivalent of a UK job centre is the *Arbeidsbureau* (AB). To find the address of the nearest office in the Netherlands look in the telephone directory or the Dutch equivalent of the Yellow Pages, *Gouden Gids*. Alternatively contact the head office of the Dutch employment service for a list of all regional employment offices.

Their address is:	Centraal Bureau voor de Arbeidsvoorziening Visseringlaan 26 Postbus 5814 2280 HV Rijswijk
Social Insurance Information Centre:	Voorlichtingscentrum Sociale Verzekering Zwaansvliet 3 1081 AP Amsterdam
For information concerning health rights:	Health Service Foreign Affairs Dept Afdeling Buitenland van het Ziekenfonds PO Box 9069 3506 GB Utrecht
For information concerning benefits:	Social Insurance Information Centre Rhijnspoorplein 1 1091 GC Amsterdam

The Ministry of Social Affairs and Employment
Anne van Hannoverstraat 4
2595 BJ The Hague

Royal Netherlands Embassy
38 Hyde Park Gate
London SW17 5DP

UK Consulate
Koningslaan 44
1075 AE Amsterdam

British Embassy
Lange Voorhout 10
2514 ED The Hague

British Council
Keizergracht 343
1016 EH Amsterdam

Netherlands–British Chamber of Commerce
Holland Trade House
Bezuidenh. 181
2594 AH The Hague

Netherlands–British Chamber of Commerce
The Dutch House
307–8 High Holborn
London WC1V 7LS

15

Portugal

Statutory Provision for Maternity Leave

- Paid maternity leave is guaranteed under the Maternity and Paternity Protection Law (law 4/84 dated 5 April 1984), amended by Decree Law 136/85 of 3 May 1985 and by Regulatory Decree 36/87 of 17 June 1987.
- There is no continuous employment requirement.
- The claimant must have made six months of social security payments prior to the birth, including the third and fourth months preceding entitlement to leave.

Entitlements

- 30 days are allowed before the birth on request, or are compulsory in cases of high clinical risk; 60 days after the birth (or 90 days in total after the birth).
- These entitlements may be increased in the event of the mother's illness.
- Maternity pay is 100 per cent of normal salary (calculated on the basis of average earnings over the six-month period prior to the second month preceding entitlement to benefit), and is paid through social security.
- 12 weeks adoption leave is available (usually taken by the mother).

Statutory Rights to Paternity Leave

- Paid paternity leave is guaranteed under the same law which deals with maternity leave (see above).
- There are no eligibility requirements.

Entitlements

- In case of the mother's physical or mental incapacity, the last 30 or 60 days of her leave may be assumed by the father. In case of her death, he assumes all her outstanding leave.
- This entitlement may not be increased.
- Maternity and paternity leave of 60 days is also guaranteed in the case of adoption.

Statutory Rights to Parental Leave

Parental leave is guaranteed under the Maternity and Paternity Protection Law (law 4/84 dated 5 April 1984).

Entitlements

The mother or father may take unpaid leave of between six months and two years to look after the child until it reaches the age of 3. There are no length of service requirements. This right, which applies to both private and public sectors, applies also to adoptive parents. Part-time leave is also possible, in which case entitlement lasts until the child reaches the age of 12.

These periods of leave may not be extended, and there are no major collective agreements at either central or sector level covering the issue. Employees have the right to return to their old job on the expiry of their leave entitlement.

Statutory Rights to Leave for Family Reasons

Paid leave for family reasons is guaranteed under Decree Law no. 674/76 of 1976 as well as law 4/84 on maternity and paternity protection.

Entitlements

- illness of spouse, or child over 10: 15 days
- illness of child under 10: 30 days
- death of close relative: 2–5 days

These periods are the maximum annual entitlement under each category.

Leave in cases of sickness is paid by social security; in cases of bereavement, it is treated as normal holiday leave.

Maternity, Paternity and Adoption Benefits

The birth or adoption of a child, as well as absence from work in order to look after children, provide entitlement, depending upon the particular case, to the following benefits:

- maternity allowance,
- paternity allowance,
- adoption allowance,
- allowance for attending to sick children,
- healthcare.

Entitlements to benefits

All working women who are covered by any type of social security scheme are entitled, on the birth of a child, to maternity allowance.

Fathers covered by a social security scheme are also entitled to paternity allowance where, after delivery of the child, the eligible mother interrupts maternity leave on account of physical or mental incapacity or death.

The adoption of a child of under 3 years of age by a man or woman likewise grants entitlement to the adoption allowance, should he or she cease employment in order to look after the child or children.

Mothers and fathers of children up to 10 years of age who are covered by the general scheme for employed persons are entitled, in the event of the sickness of, or accidents to, children or persons enjoying the same status, to the allowance for attendance to sick children.

Conditions governing the award of benefits and their duration

To be entitled to the cash benefits referred to claimants must have registered under the social security system for at least six months. For entitlement to the allowance in the case of sick children they must also, in addition to satisfying the conditions requiring registration and the payment of contributions, be exercising exclusive authority on account of the absence of the child's other parent. Moreover, the allowance is granted only to persons on low incomes.

The period during which the allowances are paid is as follows:

- maternity: 90 days,
- paternity: between 10 and 90 days,
- adoption: 60 days,
- attendance for sick children: 30 days in a year.

Level of benefits

The maternity and paternity allowance is 100 per cent of average earnings, calculated on the same basis as is the sickness allowance. The allowance payable under the special scheme for agricultural workers is also calculated on the same basis as is the sickness allowance, albeit it is a lesser amount.

The daily allowance for attendance on sick children is 65 per cent of one-thirtieth of the minimum monthly earnings of the beneficiary's sector of activity.

Family Benefits

Where a worker has specific family responsibilities the social security schemes grant various benefits:

One-off benefits are:

- birth allowance,
- marriage allowance,
- death grant,
- allowance for attendance of a third person.

Ongoing benefits are, in general:

- family allowance,
- nursing allowance.

For children with learning difficulties:

- additional grant,
- special education allowance,
- lifelong allowance,
- lifelong monthly allowance,
- allowance for attendance of a third person.

Entitlements to benefits

The birth and marriage grants are payable to claimants on the birth of a child or on the child's marriage.

The death grant entitlement is acquired on the death of the employee or of the following family members: spouse, children and persons treated on the same basis with entitlement to the family allowance and parents or grandparents dependent on the beneficiary. The children or persons treated on the same basis (stepsons, stepdaughters, adopted children, wards, etc.) provide entitlement to all ongoing benefits.

Conditions governing the award of benefits and their duration

Members of the general scheme for employed persons are granted family benefits provided that they have paid contributions, in their own name, in the previous 12 months. However, those people covered by the self-employed workers' scheme or by the special scheme for agricultural workers are granted benefits only if they have paid contributions in a regularized form.

For the parent to receive family allowance the child should not be aged over 14. However, family allowance is usually granted when children are up to the ages of 18, 22 and 25, provided that they are following secondary, intermediate or higher education, as the case may be. Family allowance is, nevertheless, paid without age limit for children who are mentally handicapped.

In the case of benefits payable on behalf of mentally handicapped children the additional allowance is paid up to the age of 24, at which age the son or daughter provides entitlement to the lifelong monthly allowance, provided that the beneficiary's total family income is of a certain level (one and a half times minimum earnings increased by 25 per cent in respect of each dependent child).

Award of the special education grant depends on whether the mentally handicapped child needs to attend a private educational establishment.

The third-person attendance allowance is paid to the severely mentally handicapped who are in receipt of an additional allowance or lifelong monthly allowance. Payment of the allowance is conditional upon the mentally handicapped person having the status of dependant.

The period during which continuous benefits are payable varies. In the case of the nursing grant benefits are provided for the first 10 months of the child's life. Once the child has attained the age of 14 the family allowance continues to be paid only if evidence continues to be provided that the child is pursuing education at one of the various levels referred to.

The additional allowance may be provided without limit of time, provided that the mentally handicapped child does not receive the social invalidity pension.

Level of benefits The level of family benefits, with the exception of the special education allowance, is fixed, the amount being updated periodically, as a rule annually.

Formalities

Family benefits are claimed from the Regional Centre by which the beneficiary is covered. In order to obtain benefits the relevant claim must be submitted and accompanied by:

- the birth certificate, the identity papers, or identity card of the child for whom the benefit is being claimed;
- proof of attendance at an educational establishment in the case of children aged over 14 if family allowance is being claimed;
- a medical certificate approved by the appropriate authorities where the child is mentally handicapped;
- medical declaration attesting that the mentally handicapped child requires special attention in the case of the special education allowance;
- certification of dependant status by the authority responsible for verifying the condition of permanent incapacity, with a view to granting of a third-person attendance allowance;
- marriage certificate if claiming the marriage allowance, or death certificate, evidence of kinship to the deceased and the receipts for funeral expenses if claiming the death grant.

Publicly Funded Childcare Provision

Of children under 3 years, 6 per cent are catered for in publicly funded childcare services; from 3 years to school age, it is 35 per cent.

Childcare provision is less widespread in rural areas than it is in the major urban districts.

Health Matters

The Portuguese national health system is run by the *Ministério de Saúde*. The award of healthcare benefits is the responsibility of the health units, which fall within the national health service. Members of the social security schemes are entitled to the most comprehensive range of healthcare. Health benefits cover essential preventative and medical care, including both general medical consultations, specialist consultations and home visits, treatment in the event of illness, pharmaceutical products, additional medical equipment such as spectacles, artificial eyes and dentures, hospital and spa treatment. There is however, a charge for treatment by a doctor in a state health centre (*Centro de Saúde*), although a pharmacist can be consulted free of charge as an alternative source of treatment of minor ailments. For individuals not paying Portuguese national insurance contributions while working, it is advisable to take out private medical insurance or face the possibility of paying the full price of treatment.

The financing of cover for workers in the event of accidents at work is entirely the responsibility of the employing undertakings concerned, as is the case regarding occupational diseases.

Sickness benefits

Claims for sickness benefits are made through the local social security offices (*Centro Regional de Segurança Social* (CRSS)) via employers. Sickness payments are not granted for the first three days of sickness (60 days in the case of self-employed workers) and can last for a maximum periods of 1,095 days, following which a worker may become covered by the invalidity protection scheme. In the case of self-employed workers the maximum period during which the allowance is granted is 365 days. The level of sickness allowance is 65 per cent of average earnings for the first six months preceding the month before that in which incapacity for work occurred.

Individuals who are in receipt of sickness benefit in another EU country may be able to transfer payment to Portugal. For further information contact the overseas branch of the Department of Social Security.

Information Points

The Portuguese equivalent of a UK job centre is a *Centro do Emprego*. These government offices are administered by the *Ministério de Emprego e Segurança Social*. Addresses can be obtained from a telephone directory or the Portuguese equivalent of Yellow Pages, *Páginas Amarelas*.

Portuguese-British Chamber of Commerce

Câmara do Comércio Luso-Britânica
Rua da Estrela 8
1200 Lisbon

For information on benefits:

Ministerio do Emprego e Segurança Social
Praça de Londres
1000 Lisbon

Department of International Relations and Social Security Conventions1
Departmento de Reloçôes Internacionais e Convençóes da Segurança Social

Rua da Junqueira
no 112-1300
300 Lisbon

Portuguese Embassy
11 Belgrave Square
London SW1Z 8PP

Portuguese Consulate-General
Silver City House
62 Brompton Road
London SW3 1BJ

The Portuguese Consulate
Alexandra Court
93a Princess Street
Manchester M1 4HT

The Portuguese Consulate
25 Bernard Street
Edinburgh EH6 6SH

British Embassy
Rua Sao Domingos à Lapa 35–37
1200 Lisbon

British Consulate
Rua da Estrela 4
1200 Lisbon

British Consulate
Largo Francisco A. Mauricio 7–1
8500 Portimao
Algarve

British Consulate
Avenida da Boavista 3072
Oporto

British Consulate
Avenida de zarco 2
Funchal

Associaçao Luso-Britanica do Porto (Anglo-Portuguese Association of Oporto)
Rua do breiner 155/165
4000 Oporto

16

Spain

Statutory Provision for Maternity Leave

- Paid maternity leave is guaranteed under Article 48 of the 1980 Workers Statute amended by law 3/1989 of 3 March 1989.
- There is no continuous employment requirement.
- The claimant must have been registered with social security for at least nine months before the birth and to have contributed for at least 180 days in the year leading up to it.

Entitlements

- A total of 16 weeks are allowed around the time of the birth distributed as requested by the employee, although at least 8 must be taken after the birth.
- This period may be extended if the woman has not sufficiently recovered for work once the 14 weeks are up.
- The woman receives 75 per cent of basic salary during maternity leave, which is calculated in the same way as benefit payable for temporary incapacity for work due to sickness.

Statutory Provision for Paternity Leave

No paternity leave is allowed as such.

- Article 37(5) of the Workers' Statute allows both male and female workers who are looking after a child up to the age of 6 to reduce their working day.
- Article 46(3) of the Workers' Statute allows both male and female workers to take unpaid leave for up to three years to look after a child.
- If both parents are in paid employment, the father is, under law 3/1989, entitled to use the last four weeks of the statutory maternity leave instead of the mother, as long as the latter's return to work does not entail any risk to her health.

Entitlements

- A father or a mother may opt for a reduced working day (with proportional cut in pay) of between two-thirds and a half of a normal day.
- If a father or mother opts for unpaid leave, this must not exceed three years, at the end of which the job may be claimed back, if a vacancy still exists.
- In the event of the mother's death, the father becomes entitled to the entire period of maternity leave.

Statutory Rights to Parental Leave

Parental leave is guaranteed under Articles 37(5) and 46(3) of the 1980 Workers Statute and the law of 3 March 1989.

Entitlements

Article 37(5) of the Workers' Statute allows both parents to reduce their working day when looking after a child up to the age of 6. The birth of further children ends the existing leave and starts a new three-year period. In all cases, such leave is unpaid. Length of service requirements are unspecified. These rights, which apply to both private and public sectors, apply also to adoptive parents. These periods of leave may not be extended. Employees have a right to return to their old job for the first year of leave, whereafter they retain only preferential rights to vacancies for the same or a similar category of job in the firm, once their leave entitlements have expired.

There are no major collective agreements at either central or sector level covering the issue.

Statutory Rights to Leave for Family Reasons

Leave for family reasons is guaranteed under Article 37(3) of the 1980 Workers' Statute.

Entitlements

Paid leave is allowed on each of the following occasions:

- illness of spouse: two to four days

- death of a close relative: two to four days
- illness of a child: two to four days
- own wedding: 14 days
- birth of a child: two days (for the father)
- moving house: one day

The length of time may be increased under collective agreement or custom and practice. It is considered as ordinary holiday entitlement for the purpose of social security.

Maternity Insurance

Maternity 180 contribution days are required during the previous year and the person in question must have been registered with the social security system at least nine months before the date on which she gives birth to the child.

Waiting period No waiting period is required before a claim takes effect where temporary incapacity for work is the result of an accident at work, an occupational disease or maternity.

Maximum period of leave The maximum period in the case of maternity is 14 weeks, eight of which are after childbirth.

Amount of benefit It is 75 per cent of salary or wage in the case of temporary incapacity for work because of an accident at work, occupational disease or maternity. In the case of temporary incapacity for work because of an ordinary accident or sickness it is 60 per cent of pay during the first 20 days and 75 per cent thereafter.

Method of payment In general, the allowance for temporary incapacity for work is paid to an employed person by his employer. Some concerns continue to pay the full wage to their workers (and accept responsibility for the difference between the wage and the benefit in respect of temporary incapacity for work).

Family Benefits

Normal family allowances A monthly allowance is awarded for each child who is either younger than 18 years or incapable of working, and is dependent upon an insured employed person or on a person who receives regular benefits from the social security scheme. The amount of the allowance is: 250 ptas; for families of four to six children, it is 313 ptas; for families of seven to nine children, 325 ptas; for families of ten or more children, 338 ptas.

Family supplement for a dependent child In order to be eligible for this supplement, the person concerned must satisfy two conditions:

1 He or she must be entitled to normal family allowances.
2 He or she must belong to one of the following categories:
   (a) persons entitled to a pension (or to temporary invalidity benefits or rehabilitation training benefits), the amount of which may not exceed the minimum amount awarded to beneficiaries of an old-age pension with a dependent spouse;
   (b) beneficiaries of an unemployment allowance awarded in the context of social assistance;
   (c) unemployed persons who are not entitled to cash benefits but who are entitled to medical benefits. The monthly amount of the family supplement is 1,050 ptas per child. Family benefits are awarded to those whose children reside in another EU member state as if they were residing in Spain.

Publicly Funded Childcare Provision

For children under 3 years it is not available. Of children from three years to school age, 70 per cent are provided for.

Services for children over 3 years up to school age include pre-school groups, nurseries, crèches and kindergartens. In many rural areas few if any services for pre-school-age children exist.

Health Matters

Medical care in Spain is administered by the *Instituto Nacional de Salud* (INSALUD). Health benefits are provided only by the social security health network or by the registered medical centres. Anyone making contributions through his or her employer to the social security system is issued with a social security card (*cartilla de la seguridad social*, also called 'medical benefit card' or 'certificate of registration') and is entitled to free hospital and medical treatment on the Spanish national health system. This also covers patients for 40 per cent of prescription charges. The only dental treatment provided under the social security system is tooth extractions.

A list of local national health centres and hospitals can be obtained from local offices of the *Instituto Nacional de la Seguridad Social* (INSS) in Spain. This is an important point because approximately 40 per cent of hospitals in Spain are private hospitals. Arranging private cover can be done either through companies in other EC member states or one of the large number of Spanish private health companies who are listed in *Paginas Amarillas* under *Clinicas Medicas*.

Accidents incurred during the course of working duties are assessed on the basis of the temporary or permanent nature of their incapacitating affect on the individual concerned. Medical benefits and rehabilitation training are provided free of charge to persons suffering the affects of a workplace injury. Anyone considered too badly injured ever to return to normal duties is given a lump sum of money as well as rehabilitation training in an occupational area of his or her choice.

Sickness benefits

Claims for sickness benefits are made through local INSS offices. Claimants should notify their employer as soon as possible about the nature of their sickness and the amount of absence they are likely to incur.

Individuals in receipt of sickness benefits in other EU countries may be able to transfer payments to Spain. Enquiries should be made to the overseas department of the Department of Social Security in their home country.

Information Points

The Spanish equivalent of a UK job centre is an *Oficina de Empleo*; these centres are run by the *Instituto Nacional de Empleo* (INEM). The state-run INEM is the only employment and recruitment agency allowed to operate in Spain for permanent work.

The Spanish Chamber of Commerce
5 Cavendish Square
London W1M 0DP

Spanish Embassy
24 Belgrave Square
London SW1X 8QA

Spanish Consulate General
20 Draycott House
London SW3 2RZ

Spanish Consulate General
1a Brook House
70 Spring Gardens
Manchester M1 3HN

Spanish Consulate General
63 North Castle street
Edinburgh EH3 3LJ

British Consulate General
Centro Colón
Marqués de la Ensenada 16
28004 Madrid

British Council
10 Spring Gardens
London SW1A 2BN

British Council
Plaza Santa Barbara 10
28010 Madrid

Instituto de España
102 Eaton Square
London SW1 4NB

British Chamber of Commerce in Spain
Plaza Santa Barbara 10
28010 Madrid

Instituto Nacional de la Seguridad
Subdireccion General de Relaciones Internacionales
Padre Damien 4
28001 Madrid

17

United Kingdom

Statutory Rights for Maternity Leave

- Paid maternity leave is guaranteed under the Social Security Act 1986.
- The principal eligibility requirement is that the claimant must have been continuously employed for at least two years before the expected week of confinement and must work at least 16 hours a week. In cases where the applicant works between 8 and 15 hours a week, five years' continuous employment is required for eligibility.

Entitlements

- Six weeks in total at 90 per cent pay followed by up to 12 weeks at a lower rate of state maternity pay is allowed. A further 22 weeks off is allowed (plus another four with a medical certificate), but the woman receives a lump-sum maternity allowance only for the first 18 weeks of this period, while the remaining period is unpaid;
- Not more than 11 weeks of the leave may be taken before the birth and not more than 29 weeks after it.
- The law allows a pregnant employee the right to reasonable time off to receive antenatal care; no length of service qualification is required.

Statutory Provision for Paternity and Parental Leave

There are no statutory provisions for paternity or parental leave.

Entitlements

There are no entitlements to paternity leave except those conceded under collective agreement. The majority of UK employers expect their employees to use holiday entitlement. Increasingly, however, around a third of large companies grant some paternity leave, two days being the most common period.

Parental leave in the UK is regulated only through negotiation or custom and practice. Personal leave in exceptional domestic circumstances (which covers parental leave) may be allowed. Parental leave is covered by no major collective agreements.

Statutory Rights to Leave for Family Reasons

There are no statutory rights.

Entitlements

Companies adopt a wide variety of approaches to special leave. National agreements rarely contain clauses on special leave other than for bereavement. Most agreements provide for special leave to be paid and for it to be awarded at management discretion. Examples of such arrangements include five days a year at Birmingham City Council and West Yorkshire Passenger Transport and ten days at Fullemploy and Oxfordshire County Council.

Maternity Grant and Maternity Allowance

Maternity grant

The maternity grant is a non-contributory lump sum payable to mothers who have been resident in Great Britiain or Northern Ireland for periods amounting in total to more than 182 days in the 52 weeks immediately preceding the date of confinement (or expected week of confinement). If a claim is made before confinement then the mother must be present in Great Britain or Northern Ireland on the date of her claim (unless at the date of the claim she is a serving member, or the wife of a serving member, of the armed forces, and she is residing with him). In certain circumstances periods abroad can count towards the more than 182 days presence test. Claims supported by a doctor's or a midwife's certificate should be made to a local social security office or in Northern Ireland to the Central Benefits Branch of the Department of Health and Social

Services any time after the fourteenth week before the baby is expected, but not later than three months after the actual date of confinement. Payment, which cannot be made earlier than 11 weeks before the expected week of confinement is made by girocheque which may be cashed in at any post office or paid into a bank. A leaflet explaining the payment conditions and giving the current amount of this benefit is available from social security offices.

Maternity allowance

Maternity allowance is paid to a woman usually for 18 weeks, starting 11 weeks before the expected week of confinement and is based on her insurance record alone. Exceptionally, an increase may be paid with maternity allowance for her husband if he is incapable of self-support. Claims supported by a doctor's or a mid-wife's certificate should be made as soon as possible after the fourteenth week before the baby is expected and not later than the eleventh week before the expected birth, otherwise some benefit may be lost. The allowance will be paid in the form of a book of orders which can be cashed in each week at a post office. Leaflets giving the current rates of benefit are available of social security offices.

Family Benefits

Qualifying conditions

Child benefits are a cash benefit payable to individuals who are responsible for one or more children under age 16, or up to 19 if the child is in full-time education (but not if he or she is on a degree or other advanced course). There are no contribution conditions, but normally the following residence condition applies: the claimant or spouse and the child are in the UK, and have lived there for more than 182 days in the past 52 weeks.

How to claim and method of payment

Claims in Great Britain should be made to the local social security office and in Northern Ireland to the Department of Health and Social Services, Child Benefit office, Castle Buildings, Stormont, Belfast BT4 3SF, enclosing the children's birth certificates if possible.

Publicly Funded Childcare Provision

Of children under 3 years, 2 per cent are catered for in publicly funded childcare services; from 3 years to school age, it is 40 per cent. (This figure is the second lowest in the European Community.)

Services include play-groups, pre-school groups and nurseries.

Health Matters

Health services in the UK are administered by the National Health Service (NHS) under the Department of Health. Free family doctor and hospital services are provided for everyone, without any national insurance qualification if they are employed or seeking work in or are ordinarily resident in the United Kingdom. In general, some charges are made towards the costs of medicines, dental services, and certain appliances and the full cost of spectacles, although some persons are exempt from some or all of these charges. Leaflets explaining the grounds for these exemptions are available from local post offices, social security offices and from some public libraries. Individuals should apply to their nearest local health centre to be registered with a national health doctor. Nearly all doctors and opticians and many dentists take part in the National Health Service. It should be noted however, that some national health doctors also practise privately so people should ensure that any treatment received is as a national health patient or they may have to meet the full cost of the treatment.

Industrial injuries benefits are payable to individuals who are unable to work as a result of an accident at work or because of one of the prescribed industrial diseases or to individuals who are able to work but have suffered a loss of faculty as a result of an accident at work or a prescribed disease. Entitlement to benefits does not depend on the amount of national insurance contributions paid, but is payable only to individuals who normally work for an employer. Individuals should notify their employer of any accident at work as soon as possible. Claims are made as for sickness benefit and benefits are paid by girocheque, which may be cashed at a post office or paid into a bank. Disablement benefit is payable if, at the end of 15 weeks from the date of the accident at work, an individual is still suffering from a loss of faculty. The amount of benefit depends on the extent of the disablement (that is, impairment of one's ability to enjoy a normal life), as assessed by a medical board.

Sickness benefits

Most employees are entitled to statutory sick pay (SSP) from that employer for periods when illness makes them incapable of work. SSP is paid instead of sickness benefit and sickness benefit cannot be paid for periods when an employer is liable to pay SSP. Employers are liable to pay SSP for a maximum of eight weeks in a tax year or in a period of incapacity which spans two tax years. Certain people who work for an employer are not covered by the SSP scheme e.g. those over the retirement pension age, as they may claim state sickness benefit. Individuals can claim cash sickness benefits when they are incapable of work because of illness or disability if the period of illness is four days or more and they are not entitled to payment of SSP from an employer for that period. No benefit is payable for the first three days of incapacity. If individuals are already in receipt of state sickness benefits in another EU country they may be able to transfer these payments to the UK.

Information Points

Advisory, Conciliation and Arbitration Service Regional Offices (ACAS):

Northern Region
Westgate House
Westgate Road
Newcastle upon Tyne NE1 1TJ

Yorkshire and Humberside Region
Commerce House
St Alban's Place
Leeds LS2 8HH

South-east Region
Westminster House
125 Fleet Road
Fleet
Aldershot
Hampshire GU13 8PD

South-west Region
Regent House
27a Regent Street
Clifton
Bristol BS8 4HR

London Region
Clifton House
83 Euston Road
London NW1 2RB

Midlands Region
Leonard House
319–323 Bradford Street
Birmingham B5 6ET

Nottingham Office
Anderson House
Clinton Avenue
Nottingham NG5 1AW

North-west Region
Boulton House
17 Chorlton Street
Manchester M1 3HY

Merseyside Office
Cressington House
249 St Mary's Road
Garston
Liverpool L19 0NF

Scotland
Franborough House
123 Bothwell Street
Glasgow G2 7JR

Wales
Phase 1
Ty Glas Road
Llanishen
Cardiff CF4 5PH

British Association for Early Childhood Education (BAECE)
111 City View House
463 Bethnal Green Road
London E2 9QH

BAECE in Scotland
Albion
Souterford Road
Inverurie AB51 9TP

Childcare Association
8 Talbot Road
London N6 4QR

Child Care Cheques
Mercer Fraser
Metropolitan House Northgate
Chichester
West Sussex PO19 1BE

Childcare Network
c/o Mr Peter Moss
Thomas Coran Research Unit
University of London
Institute of Education
41 Brunswick Square
London WC1N 1AZ

Childcare Now (Scotland)
3 Hopeward Mews
Dalgety Bay
Fife KY11 5TB

Childcare Solutions
50 Vauxhall Bridge Road
London SW1V 2RS

Childcare Vouchers
50 Vauxhall Bridge Road
London SW1V 2RS

Commission of the European Communities
Jean Monnet House
8 Storey's Gate
London SW1P 3AT

Confederation of British Industry (CBI)
Centre Point
103 New Oxford Street
London WC1A IDU

Daycare Trust
Wesley House
4 Wild Court
London WC2B 5AU

Department of Employment
Caxton House
Tothill Street
London SW1H 9NF

Department of Health
International Section
Eileen House
80–94 Newington Causeway
London SE1 6EF

Equal Opportunities Commission
Overseas House
Quay Street
Manchester M3 3HN

Family Centre Network
c/o NCVCCO
National Children's Bureau
8 Wakley Street
London EC1V 7QE

Federation of Recruitment and Employment Services
36 Mortimer Street
London W1N 7RB

Health and Safety Executive Information Centre
Broad Lane
Sheffield S3 7HQ

Health and Safety Executive Information Centre
Baynards House
1 Chepstow Place
Westbourne Grove
London W2 4TF

Institute of Personnel Management
IPM House
Camp House
Wimbledon
London SW19 4UX

Kids Clubs Network
279–281 Whitechapel Road
London E1 1BY

Maternity Alliance
15 Britannia Street
London WC1X 9JP

Mobile Projects Association Scotland
12 Picardy Place
Edinburgh EH1 3JT

National Childcare Campaign/ Childcare Now
Wesley House
4 Wild Court
London WC2B 5AU

National Childminding Association
8 Mason's Hill
Bromley
Kent BR2 9EY

National Consumer Council (NCC)
20 Grosvenor Gardens
London SW1W 0DH

National Out-of-School Alliance
Oxford House
Derbyshire Street
London E2 6HG

National Playbus Association
Unit G
Arnos Castle Estate
Junction Road
Brislington
Bristol BS4 3JP

Pre-school Playgroups Association
61–63 Kings Cross Road
London WC1X 9LL

Scottish Association of Family Centres
Broxburn Family Centre
1–3 Henderson Place
Broxburn EH52 6EY

Scottish Child and Family Alliance (SCAFA)
55 Albany Street
Edinburgh EH1 3QY

Scottish Childminding Association
17 Middleton Drive
Milngavie
Glasgow G5 3SB

Scottish Pre-school Play Association
14 Elliott Place
Glasgow G3 8EP

Strathclyde After School Care Association
39 Hope Street
Glasgow G2 6HE

Training, Enterprise and Education Directorate (TEED)
Department of Employment
Moorfoot
Sheffield S1 4PQ
(For information on the local TEC)

Trades Union Congress (TUC)
Congress House
23–28 Gt Russell Street
London WC1B 3LS

Voluntary Organizations Liaison Council for Under Fives (VOLCUF)
77 Holloway Road
London N7 8JZ

Working for Childcare
77 Holloway Road
London N7 8JZ

Appendix 1
Glossary of Terms

Note: Although the majority of terms included in this glossary could relate to systems in operation across the EU, the specific information is biased towards UK provision and readers in the UK.

Arbitration

The process of resolving disputes by bringing in a third party.

Childminders

For parents who want their child to be looked after in a home setting, engaging the services of a childminder is one option. A childminder looks after a child in her own home on a regular basis. The social services/social work department may register a childminder to look after a maximum of six children under the age of 8, including her own. She never looks after more than 3 children under the age of 5.

Childminders can provide full-time, part-time and flexible day-care. For full-time care, they usually take children between 8 a.m. and 6 p.m.

Childminders can offer care in the child's own neighbourhood, and an opportunity to form friendships that continue through play-group, nursery and on to school. Childminders may take and collect children who go to a play-group, and may continue to look after school-age children before and after school and in the school holidays.

Childminders and parents need to have a clear understanding about their arrangements for such matters as fees, times for leaving and collecting the child, arrangements for sickness (child, parent or childminder), holidays and so on. Childminders should have a Public Liability insurance policy. A written contract is the best foundation for a good relationship. The National Childminding Association has a sample contract for sale.

Collective agreement

An agreement reached between management and trade unions which covers a particular working group.

Conciliation

The process of resolving disputes by involving a third party who does not make a decision but tries to aid the process of reaching agreements.

Confinement

Confinement means the birth of a live child or the birth of a child whether living or dead after 28 weeks of pregnancy. A woman who suffers a miscarriage before the end of the twenty-eighth week of pregnancy and is absent from work is not absent because of confinement.

Confirmation of intention to return

An employer has the right during a woman's maternity leave to seek confirmation of her intention to return to work. Note: an employee is not bound to give notice to terminate her existing contract of employment.

Continuous service

Women who want to satisfy the continuous service rule must have been employed for at least 26 'Sunday to Saturday' weeks continuing into the qualifying week (QW). Employment for just part of the QW is enough for it to count as one of these weeks. Where a woman has been with her employer for 26 weeks only, the first week need not be a complete 'Sunday to Saturday' week. Employment for any part of that week will suffice.

Where in any week there is no contract for the whole or part of that week because the woman is absent from work for certain reasons, and then returns to work, that week shall be as part of her continuous period of employment, even where no contract of service exists during that week. The reasons are:

1 She is incapable of work owing to sickness or injury (subject to an upper limit of 26 consecutive weeks); or
2 She is absent from work on account of temporary cessation of work; or
3 She is absent from work in circumstances such that, by custom or arrangement she is regarded as continuing in employment; or
4 She is absent from work wholly or partly because of pregnancy or confinement (subject to an upper limit of 26 weeks).

Where a woman takes statutory maternity leave and returns to work in accordance with the statutory maternity rules, continuity of service is preserved for the whole period of absence.

Note that the period spent by trainees on certain (but not all) government training schemes does not count towards a period of continuous employment because the trainees are not employees (that is, they are not working under a contract of employment). Further information and advice on this matter may be obtained from any regional office of the Advisory, Conciliation and Arbitration Service, the addresses of which are given at the end of Chapter 17.

Contract of employment

The legal relationship between employers and employees, governing what an employee must do and what he or she must receive in conditions and wages.

Discrimination

Occurs when one person or group of people is treated less fairly than another group, usually on the grounds of sex or race.

Dismissal

The ending of an employee's employment with an organization. The procedure for dismissing an employee must be fair; for example, several warnings must be given to an employee before he or she is dismissed.

Employee

An employee is the person whose earnings attract a liability for employers' Class 1 National Insurance contributions, or would do if they were high enough.

Employer

Person liable to pay employer's share of Class 1 contributions.

Expected week of confinement (EWC)

The expected week of confinement is the week in which a pregnant woman's baby is due to be born. It is provided on the maternity certificate form MAT B1, and given to her employer as a proof of her pregnancy.

Industrial tribunal

An industrial tribunal is an informal hearing which deals with employment matters. The tribunal panel consists of a chairperson who is legally qualified, and two lay persons, one representing the employer and one the employee. Industrial tribunal hearings are conducted informally and in a way that makes it easy for both parties to present their own case if they wish. There is no legal aid available for tribunals, although both parties may claim travelling and other expenses within certain limits, including loss of earnings.

Job sharing

This means two people agreeing to share one full-time job. Normally the hours are divided in half, either mornings and afternoons, or half a week each.

Nannies

A nanny looks after a child in the child's own home. Trained nannies have a recognized childcare qualification. Nannies take complete charge of the child in the absence of the parents. They should be responsible for every aspect of the child's care, including cleaning and tidying up after the child, cleaning the child's room, cooking the child's meals and doing their washing and ironing. However nannies do not generally carry out other housework beyond taking care of their own room, if they live in.

Employing a nanny, like childminding, offers care in the child's own neighbourhood with an opportunity to take part in local activities and form friendships that continue through play-group, nursery and on to school.

Working arrangements can be flexible. Some nannies live with the family full-time which can include some weekend working. Others are employed daily. Sometimes more than one family shares a nanny for their children. If more than two sets of parents arrange to share a nanny, the nanny must register with the social services/social work department in the same way as a childminder must. It is important to have a contract of employment which clearly states the hours of work and the jobs the nanny is expected to do. Most employment agencies have their own contract for nannies.

Nursery education

Community nurseries are run by non-profit making groups or community businesses. Some have a project name (Stepping Stones, for example) rather than calling themselves a nursery. While some are specifically funded to enable single parents to work or study, this is not always the case. There are fewer than 50 community nurseries in the UK.

Day nurseries provide care for young children up to the age of 5. They may be run by local authorities, community groups, private commercial companies or workplaces, or by a partnership between employers and local authorities or employers and community groups. There should always be an adult for every eight children aged from about 3 to 5. If the nursery has children younger than 3 years old, the ratio of adults to children is higher.

Occasionally day nurseries are called children's centres, and are usually run by social services or social work departments. They offer places to single parents or to families whose circumstances mean that children need all-day care. Individuals who think they may qualify for a place should contact their local social services/social work department.

Nurseries have to have special arrangements for looking after children under the age of 2 and not all nurseries will accept young babies.

Most nurseries offering full daycare are open from 8 a.m. until 6 p.m. They are usually open all year, but sometimes close for a week or two in the summer and at Christmas. Children can sometimes attend part time.

Private nursery schools must register with social services/social work departments if they take children from 3 to 5 years old. Standards of premises, equipment and staffing (including both members of staff and their qualifications) are the same as for day nurseries. If more than five pupils over the age of 5 attend the school, it must register as an independent school. It is then run under the regulations which apply to nursery classes and schools, with a qualified teacher in every class as well as a nursery assistant.

Workplace nurseries are run by businesses and other organizations, and provide daycare for the children of employees.

Occasional care

Crèches Some people use the term 'crèche' for any kind of nursery, but it is best to use it only for services which provide supervised childcare for an occasional, limited period of time. Crèches enable parents and carers to follow other activities on the same premises, though not necessarily in the same room, as the child.

Some crèches are a permanent feature, for example, the crèches provided in shopping centres, leisure centres and colleges. These have to register as full-day nurseries. Other crèches are organized for a special event, such as a conference, and if used for fewer than six days a year, count as occasional daycare and do not have to conform to the same standards as a nursery.

The children in a crèche are unlikely to be a group that is regularly cared for together. The age range may be much wider than is normally the case in childcare settings. Crèches often care for young babies and infants and children up to 12 or 13. The time that they operate for can vary from the very short (such as 30 minutes, in a hospital out-patients crèche) to very long (for example, several days, in a crèche serving a conference).

Crèche premises will often be temporary and may not always be ideal. However, they should at least be roomy, warm and clean. Responsible organizers will always make sure that they are secure and safe.

Parent and toddler groups These meet for an hour or two once or twice a week. The parent or carer always stays with the child but some groups also have a paid helper to organize and run activities.

Playbuses Playbuses provide mobile community activities. So, as, it travels around the neighbourhood, you may find your local playbus offering play-groups, parent and toddler groups, crèches for special events and other activities. Some playbuses organize sessions for particular groups, such as disabled children. There may be different activities on each day of the week.

Play-groups Nearly half of all 3- to 4-year-olds go to play-groups in their local community. For the child, going to play-group means discovering a safe stimulating place in which to learn with other children, in the company of friendly adults. There should always be an adult for every eight children in the playgroup.

Although most play-groups open for sessions – half a day at a time, not necessarily every day of the week – many in England now offer extended or full-day care to meet the needs of working parents. Most play-groups close during the school holidays, although those catering for working parents may stay open.

Most children who go to playgroups begin when they are 3 years old, but some children of 2½ are accepted. Parents are encouraged to be actively involved in, and responsible for, running playgroups, although there are almost always paid playleaders to organise and run activities.

Out-of-school care for school-age children

'Out of school' is defined as time when children are not formally attending school.

'Care' is defined as providing for the needs of children, including play, safety and security, both for leisure and educational purposes.

'Out-of-school care' is defined as the care provided for children outside of their school attendance.

'Out-of-school care schemes provide safe and creative play opportunities for school-age children in a home-from-home atmosphere. Schemes must ensure that children are provided with suitable snacks or meals. They may be run by the local authority, voluntary or community groups, or private companies. The scheme must be registered with the local social services/social work department if children under 8 attend.

Holiday play-schemes Holiday schemes cater for children during the school holidays and sometimes at half-term holidays. They operate like out-of-school clubs, but far more schemes are set up for holidays, especially in the summer.

Open access play-schemes This describes schemes such as adventure playgrounds. There is no limit on the numbers of children who attend and children come and go as they please. There are no formal arrangements for bringing or collecting children and no register to record who is present. They are generally open all day in the holiday and at half term.

Out-of-school clubs Out of school clubs offer care for school-age children from the end of the school day for two or three hours and sometimes before school starts. They are often on school premises. A quiet room should be provided, where children can relax or play quietly, as well as a play room for more lively activities. There is a limit on the numbers of children who may attend based on the size and facilities of the premises. Children must be taken and collected by an adult and a register of the children attending must be kept. There should always be an adult for every eight children under 8.

Parental leave

Parental leave is defined in Articles 1 and 4 of the draft EU directive on parental leave as a period of leave to look after a child, available to employees (who can be either parent) after (but not necessarily immediately after) maternity leave has expired. The European Commission's proposal for a directive on parental leave and leave for family reasons was introduced in 1986 at the same time as the Council of Ministers approved the second community action programme on the promotion of equal opportunities for women (1986–90). Progress on this front has been slow, however, with the proposed directive no nearer coming into force now than it was in 1986.

Partnership

Partnership in childcare occurs when several organizations are brought together to share provision.

Paternity leave

Paternity leave is the time off work that is the right of fathers to take around the time of the birth of their children. It ranges within its provision both within the UK and the EU member states. Denmark is by far the most generous in its provision for paternity leave. In other countries, including the UK, many employers increasingly provide two to three days' leave to fathers around the time of the birth of their child.

Positive action

Under the terms of the UK's Sex Discrimination Act and the equivalent laws in other EU member states, employers can take action to encourage women to take up work previously done on the whole by men only. The main argument for positive action is that deep-seated attitudes and the social or economic obstacles facing disadvantaged groups cannot be overcome simply by legislating for formal equality of opportunity. To create real equality of opportunity it is necessary to make it easier for members of certain groups to gain education and to progress in occupations previously closed to them.

Qualifying week (QW)

A pregnant employee's qualifying week is the fifteenth week before her expected week of confinement. An employee has to have worked for the same employer for 26 consecutive weeks running into the QW in order to be considered for statutory maternity pay.

Statutory maternity leave

Throughout the European Union this is a universal right for all employed women. It applies to a pregnant employee's right to return to work with the same employer. In all but one member state (the UK) the full period of leave, regardless of length of employment, is covered by benefits of between 70 and 80 per cent of earnings.

To qualify for statutory maternity leave in the UK a woman must be employed by the same employer for at least two years by the end of the twelfth week before the expected date of birth (if she works at least 16 hours a week), but for five years if she works for 8 to 16 hours per week. As a result of these conditions a large number of women in the UK are excluded from the right to return to work.

Statutory Maternity Pay

Statutory Maternity Pay (SMP) was introduced in the UK on 6 April 1987. It is payable by employers to employees who take maternity leave or leave employment because of pregnancy or confinement and who satisfy certain qualifying conditions. SMP is payable at a lower and a higher rate.

SMP replaced the old system of maternity provision under which women could receive maternity allowance from the state and, where applicable, maternity pay from their employers. Although this system no longer operates, state maternity allowance is still available (subject to certain conditions) to women who are not entitled to receive SMP.

Like statutory sick pay, where statutory maternity pay is properly paid, employees can reclaim the amount from the government by way of deductions from National Insurance contributions. Where a woman is eligible to receive SMP she should be paid it whether or not she is entitled to return to work after her baby is born.

Eligibility SMP is payable by employers to employees. For the purposes of the scheme, an employee is defined as a person whose earnings attract a liability for employer's Class 1 National Insurance contributions (or would if they were high enough) and an employer is defined as someone who is liable to pay the employer's share of Class 1 National Insurance contributions.

In order for a pregnant employee to qualify she must:

1 have been continuously employed by her employer for at least 26 weeks (irrespective of the number of hours worked) ending with the fifteenth week before the expected week of confinement (EWC). This fifteenth week is known as the qualifying week (QW);
2 have average weekly earnings of not less than the lower earnings limit for the payment of NI contributions which is in force during her QW;
3 still be pregnant at the eleventh week before the EWC, or have already been confined;
4 have stopped working for her employer wholly or partly because of pregnancy or confinement;
5 provide her employer with notice of her maternity absence;
6 provide her employer with evidence of her EWC.

Terms and conditions

What is expected of an employee and what an employee can expect from working for an organization, for instance: basic payment rates, holidays, overtime pay.

The right to return

An employee who is absent from work wholly or partly because of confinement is entitled to return to work. The right is available to an employee whether or not a contract of employment subsists during her absence, assuming she meets the qualifying rules. Whether or not a woman qualifies for the statutory right to return is assessed at the eleventh week before her expected week of confinement. To qualify she must:

1 have accumulated two years' continuous service, being employed for at least 16 hours per week (or five years' continuous service, being employed for at least 8 but less than 16 hours per week) by the beginning of the eleventh week before the expected week of confinement; and
2 still be employed by her employer at that time. This means that she must still have a contract of employment but she does not necessarily have to be at work, i.e. she could qualify if she were off sick.

Notifying her employer In addition to the qualifying criteria above, the right to return after is contingent on the employee complying with strict notification rules. She must inform her employer in writing at least 21 days before the start of the absence (or if this is not reasonably practicable, as soon as reasonably practicable):

1 that she will be absent from work because of pregnancy or confinement; and
2 that she intends to return to work; and
3 the expected week of confinement.

Restrictions on the right to return An employee's right to return may be restricted in the following circumstances:

1 If her former job is no longer available because of redundancy, her employer must offer her suitable alternative work, if the employer has any. Otherwise the dismissal will be unfair. If the employer cannot offer suitable alternative work, she may be entitled to redundancy pay, but if she unreasonably refuses a suitable offer, she may forfeit her right to redundancy pay.
2 If the employer can satisfy an industrial tribunal that he or she finds it not reasonably practicable, for a reason other than redundancy, to offer the employee back her original job, and has instead offered available, suitable alternative work, and can show that the employee unreasonably rejected the offer, the failure to permit her return to her original job will not be treated as a dismissal; any claim of unfair dismissal would therefore fail;
3 If the employer can satisfy an industrial tribunal that the total number of employees employed by that employer added to the number employed by any associated employer immediately before the beginning of her maternity absence was five or less, and that it is not reasonably practicable for the employer (or an associated employer) to take her back in her old job or to offer her suitable alternative work, the failure to permit her return will not be treated as a dismissal; any claim of unfair dismissal would therefore fail.

Suitable alternative work in these three circumstances means work that is both suitable and appropriate for the employee, and of which the terms, conditions and location are not substantially less favourable than those of her employment before her maternity absence.

If the employer fails to permit the employee to return to her previous job, subject to the restrictions outlined above, that failure will be treated as dismissal. The reason for her employer's failure to allow her to return will be treated as the reason for the dismissal. The woman may complain to an industrial tribunal that she was unfairly dismissed on the date of the dismissal. If the industrial tribunal finds the complaint justified, it may order the employer to reinstate the employee in her old job, or to re-engage her in a suitable alternative one. If neither reinstatement not re-engagement is practicable, or the employee does not want it, the industrial tribunal can instead make a cash award in compensation. The complaint should be made within three months of the day she intended to return to work. The employee can also complain to an industrial tribunal that the employer has failed to pay the redundancy payment due to her, if she was dismissed because of redundancy.

Time off for antenatal care

An employee who is pregnant and has made an appointment to receive antenatal care on the advice of a registered medical practitioner, registered midwife or registered health worker, has the right to take time off with pay to keep the appointment. The employer must not unreasonably refuse the request for time off but he or she is entitled to ask that the woman provides evidence of the appointment and (except for the first appointment) produces a certificate stating that she is pregnant. This right applies to all pregnant employees; it does not depend upon the number of hours worked or length of service. An employee who is taking time off is entitled to be paid for the absence at the appropriate hourly rate.

A woman may complain to an industrial tribunal that her employer has unreasonably refused to allow her to take time off for antenatal care or has failed to pay her the whole or part of the amount due. The complaint must be presented within three months of the date of the appointment unless it was not reasonably practicable to do so. Where a tribunal upholds a complaint it must make a declaration to that effect and order the employer to pay the amount due to her or the amount she would have been entitled to had the time off not been refused.

Time off for family responsibilities

This embodies the right to paid or unpaid leave from work for family reasons. The EU draft directive for parental leave and time off for family responsibilities gives four specific reasons that could justify time off: (1) illness of a spouse; (2) death of a near relative; (3) death of a child; (4) illness of a child or the person caring for a child.

Many countries allow leave for many reasons not specifically covered in the draft directive. Examples include: the employee's own wedding (Belgium, France, Luxembourg, Spain); moving house (Luxembourg and Spain); or the illness of a close relative (Belgium); visits to a child's school (Greece); a first Holy Communion (Belgium); and own wedding anniversary (Germany).

Usually time off is permitted on each occasion that circumstances arise. An exception is Greece, which places an upper limit on the number of days of leave for family reasons as six per year.

Welfare benefits

There are three types of welfare benefits:

Non-contributory benefits are those that an individual can claim simply because he or she falls into a certain category, such as that of simple parent.

Contributory benefits can be claimed only if enough National Insurance contributions have been paid. These benefits include unemployment benefit.

Means-tested benefits are special need payments. Whether a person is entitled to them depends on his or her income, outgoings and savings, in other words their 'means'. They include income support and housing benefits.

Appendix 2
European Union Law

Outlined below are summaries of the different types of European Union measures in use.

Directives

A directive is a European Union law which is legally binding on all member states. In most cases this means that national legislation has to be proposed or current laws have to be changed in order that they comply with the directive's requirements.

Regulations

A regulation is a law which is binding in all member states but does not require any national legislation to be implemented.

Decisions

Decisions can be issued by the Council of Ministers or by the European Commission. They are legally binding on those to whom they are addressed. They may be addressed either to a member state, a company, or an individual.

Recommendations and opinions

Neither recommendations nor opinions have any legally binding effect. They are not laws. Instead, they state the view of the institution that issues them (in general, the European Commission), and they may encourage or suggest that certain action be taken.

Appendix 3
European Union Address List

Consumers' organizations

Confederation of Family Organizations in the EU (COFACE)	Confederation des Organisations Familiales de la CE Rue de Londres 17 B-1050 Brussels
European Community of Consumer Co-operatives (EURO COOP)	Communauté Européenne des Co-operatives de Consommateurs Rue Archimede 17A Bte 2 B-1040 Brussels
The European Consumers' Organization	Bureau Européen des Unions de Consommateurs (BEUC) Avenue de Tervueren 36 Bte 4, B-1040 Brussels
	Equal Opportunities Unit Rue de la Loi 200 1049 Brussels
European Commission Childcare Network	c/o Scottish Child and Family Alliance 55 Albany Street Edinburgh Eh1 3QY

Employers' organizations

Confederation Européenes des Cadres	Rion-Point Schuman 9 Bte 4 B-1040 Brussels

European Federation of Employers in Public Services (EUROFEDOP)

Federation Européene du Personnel des Services Publics
Rue de Trèves 33
B-1040 Brussels

European Round Table of Industrialists

Rue Grimard 15
B-1040 Brussels

Union of Industrial and Employers' Confederation of Europe (UNICE)

Union des Confederations de l'Industrie et des Employeurs d'Europe
Rue Joseph II 40
Bte 4
B-1040 Brussels

Appendix 4

Pregnancy: Employers' and Employees' Checklist

Risks to Pregnant Workers

Employers ought to assess the risks to pregnant workers and take steps to avoid problems. Employers should remember that the foetus is particularly vulnerable early in pregnancy, when the woman might not even know she is pregnant. Pregnant women should avoid heavy lifting and long periods of continuous standing and are not allowed to work with lead or in jobs that would expose them to levels of radiation above specified limits. Pregnant women must be given time off for antenatal appointments.

A non-exhaustive list of agents, processes and working conditions that must be assessed by the employer is:

Physical agents: those regarded as causing foetal lesions or likely to disrupt placental attachment, particularly shocks, vibration or movement; handling of loads entailing risks; noise; ionizing radiation; non-ionizing radiation; extremes of cold and heat; movements or postures; travelling; and mental and physical fatigue. Work in hyperbaric atmospheres, such as pressurized enclosures and underwater diving are also disallowed.

Biological agents: risk groups 2, 3 and 4 within the meaning of Directive 90/679/EEC, in so far as it is known that they endanger the health of the woman or foetus; toxoplasma, rubella virus (unless immunized).

Chemical agents: substances labelled R40, R45, R46 AND R47; chemical agents in annex 1 to Directive 90/394/EEC; mercury and mercury derivatives, lead and lead derivatives.

Note: Breastfeeding workers must not be exposed (Annex 2 of the directive) to the following:

- chemical agents: lead and lead derivatives;
- working conditions: underground mining work.

Protecting Pregnant Employees' Health

In the UK, the Employment Protection (Consolidation) Act 1978, states that all pregnant employees have the right to paid time off for antenatal care, however recently they started their job or whatever hours they work. Antenatal care includes classes to help women prepare for the birth of the baby as well as hospital check-ups.

Changing an employee's work

If an employee is doing work that is dangerous or illegal during pregnancy (e.g. working with certain chemicals or with X-rays) the employer should move her to another job within the workplace. Employers may need to accommodate a pregnant employee in another job if she is doing heavy lifting or may not be able to work adequately at her usual job because of pregnancy. Not all workers qualify automatically to be moved to an alternative job. Workers have the right to move if they have worked for the same employer for two years (at or over 16 hours a week) or five years (at least 8 but less than 16 hours a week). If the worker has the right, she must be offered an alternative job on similar terms and conditions to her original work.

Display screen equipment

There has been considerable concern about the higher levels of miscarriage and birth defects reported among some groups of VDU users. However, reliable studies have been unable to demonstrate any link between miscarriage or birth defects and VDUs. The National Radiological Protection Board considers that VDU radiation emissions do not put unborn children at risk. Pregnant women need not stop work with VDUs. However, to avoid problems caused by anxiety, women who are pregnant or planning children and worried about working with VDUs are advised to talk to their doctors.

The UK-based Trades Union Congress (TUC) has produced a booklet entitled *Guidelines on VDUs* which argues that VDU work can produce a wide range of physical and psychological health problems among operators, although these may often be attributable to the work environment and job design rather than the machines themselves. The TUC argues that pregnant women should have the right, on demand, to transfer to non-VDU work.

Faced with research that fails to confirm any ill-health effects, the trade union response has been that the burden should be upon employers to demonstrate that display screen equipment is harmless, rather than on employees to prove that it is hazardous. Many British unions are following the example of some Swedish workplaces, and, recognizing that most damage to the foetus occurs in the early stages of pregnancy, argue that women who are planning to become pregnant should have the right to transfer to non-display screen equipment work for a temporary period.

Assessment Guide for Employers

Listed below are a number of practical steps to help employers carry out their obligations to pregnant employees. Employers should analyse working areas and, where risks are found, take appropriate remedial action. In practice this process needs to include the following steps:

- planning the assessment;
- carrying out the assessment;
- analysis of findings;
- implementing remedial action;
- monitoring effectiveness.

Planning the assessment Employers and pregnant employees should familiarize themselves with the health and safety regulations and guidance procedures which apply to their particular industry or occupation. It is good practice to involve employees in the assessment and to ensure that:

- they receive health and safety training;
- they receive information about plans to assess work areas and take appropriate action to combat any risks found;

- they are informed about their entitlements to transfer to alternative jobs (where applicable) and to time off work to attend antenatal appointments;
- they are informed about any other changes of activity.

Carrying out the assessment The assessment of a work area is best carried out on the basis of a checklist completed by the employer, employee, trade union or staff association representative (depending on the size of the organization), or by staff appointed by an employer to make assessments in consulation with the employee. Those involved in making the assessment should have had sufficient training to understand the significance of the responses and what remedial action to take.

Analysis of findings A person or working party should be appointed to analyse and evaluate the results of an assessment.

Implemanting remedial action Any corrective action that can be implemented immediately should be carried out. Further action should be decided upon and the activities to implement improvement timetabled.

Monitoring effectiveness The long-term effectiveness and success of any corrective action can only be assessed by regular monitoring. Depending on the size and nature of an organization, it might include some or all of the following methods:

- collecting statistics;
- handing out questionnaires and forms to assess the staff's feelings and reactions;
- reviewing working activities and conditions regularly.

Main points for a checklist

- Identify workers who may be at risk.
- Circulate a questionnaire to employees.
- Make a short written report and circulate it to colleagues or safety committees.
- Agree a forward programme of action, and examine ways of eliminating problem working methods for pregnant employees.
- Agree appropriate weight ranges for particular manual handling tasks, and make a list of all relevant factors, including:
  (a) nature of load

(b) its weight
(c) working conditions
(d) frequency of handling; and
(e) skills, experience and any relevant personal factors

- Make sure everyone understands the need for safe manual handling techniques, examine the need for retraining.
- Re-survey the workplace regularly to pinpoint manual handling hazards and review accident and ill health records for signs of manual handling injury.

Organizational arrangments

- Make sure there is good training of managers, supervisors and employees.
- Supervisors should be on the look out for symptons and overwork;
- Sensitive reporting procedures are essential if symptons are to be caught before damage sets in and employees are not to be afraid of losing their jobs if they do report symptons.

Working conditions

- Assess the amount of time spent by employees on a particular task, for example, using a display screen.
- Try to ensure that employees do not suffer from unnecessary fatigue or stress; if they do, consider transferring them to another job.
- Adjust chairs to enable the user to find a comfortable position.
- Ensure that employees' feet touch the floor or a footrest.
- Use adjustable keyboards and screens to allow users to find comfortable positions.

Appendix 5

Summary: Maternity, Paternity and Parental Rights in EU Member States

Country	*Maternity leave*	*Maternity pay*
Belgium	14 weeks altogether, of which 8 weeks must be taken after the birth, and 6 weeks can be taken before or after the birth	100% of earnings for the first 1–4 weeks, 85 per cent for next 10 weeks.
Denmark	4 weeks before the birth, 14 weeks after with a further 10 weeks optional to be taken by the father or mother	For manual works, 90% of salary for 28 weeks. Non-manual workers at least 50% of salary for 21 weeks up to a specified limit.
France	16 weeks altogether, 6 before the birth; 18 weeks extra for multiple births and 28 weeks extra for repeated multiple births. For third and subsequent births women may have an extra 8 weeks before the birth and 18 weeks extra after.	84% of earnings
Germany	14 weeks altogether, 6 weeks before the birth and 8 after (12 for multiple or premature births)	100% of average earnings or fixed sum

Country	*Maternity leave*	*Maternity pay*
Greece	15 weeks altogether, 6 weeks before the birth	100% of earnings
Ireland	14 weeks altogether, 4 weeks before the birth; 4 weeks extra which is unpaid	70% of earnings plus 30% as social security. Public sector 100% of earnings
Italy	20 weeks altogether, 8 weeks before the birth. Public sector workers may apply for 4 weeks extra paid maternity leave.	80% of earnings
Luxembourg	16 weeks altogether, 8 weeks before and 8 weeks after the birth (12 for multiple births and breastfeeding)	100% of earnings
The Netherlands	12 weeks officially, though most women take 16 weeks altogether; 4–6 weeks before and 10–12 weeks after the birth	100% of earnings
Portugal	90 days altogether; 60 days after the birth, the rest can be taken before or after the birth. 12 weeks adoption leave available	100% of earnings
Spain	16 weeks altogether; 6 weeks can be taken before or after the birth. For adoption, 8 weeks if the child is under 9 months old, 6 weeks for 9 months–15 years old	75% of earnings
UK	40 weeks altogether. Can take up to 11 before the birth and 29 weeks after	90% of earnings for 6 weeks followed by flat rate payment for 12 weeks. The rest unpaid

Country	*Maternity leave*	*Maternity pay*
Belgium	None, but workers can take leave for family or personal reasons	Public sector employees entitled to 4 days; in the private sector the men are entitled to 2 days.
Denmark	10 weeks with 90% of earnings; 100% with collective agreement in public sector. Private sector, 14 weeks with full pay	2 weeks at 90% of earnings (100% under collective agreement)
France	Until the child is 3. No payment unless 3 or more children	Three days to be taken in period of 2 weeks around the date of the birth
Germany	Up to 12 months leave on the birth on adoption of a child. For civil servants, 3 years leave (for children born after 31/12/91) of which 2 years is paid. First 6 months at flat rate regardless of income; remaining 18 months at reduced rate depending on family income.	None
Greece	3 months for each parent, 6 months for lone parents, unpaid until child is 2½ years old	None
Ireland	None	None
Italy	6 months at 30% of earnings during child's first year	None
Luxembourg	Public sector workers have the right to a year's unpaid leave	Fathers entitled to two days' leave under 'personal leave' entitlement

Country	*Maternity leave*	*Maternity pay*
The Netherlands	Available on an unpaid part-time basis for a maximum of 6 months, to both parents	2 days by collective agreement
Portugal	24 months unpaid	Paternity leave is guaranteed if the mother is incapacitated.
Spain	3 years' unpaid leave per child's	None, but provision made for both parents to take up to 3 years' unpaid leave to look after child. If both parents are in paid employment, the father is entitled to the last 4 weeks of the statutory maternity leave instead of the mother.
UK	None	None

Index